"We learned to play and work and love with an intensity that drew us out of ourselves, beyond ourselves, to dream and achieve more than we imagined possible."

—Demi Lockett Prentis, *Mystic,* 1963–72

MARIMETA

SLEEPAWAY

SLEEPAWAY

The Girls of Summer and the Camps They Love

BY LAURIE SUSAN KAHN

WORKMAN PUBLISHING · NEW YORK

Library of Congress Cataloging-in-Publication Data
Kahn, Laurie Susan.
Sleepaway: The girls of summer and the camps they love / by Laurie Susan Kahn.
ISBN 0-7611-2691-0
1. Camps for girls—United States—Miscellanea.
I. Title.
GV197.G5K35 2003
796.54'082—dc21   2003041052

Workman books are available at special discounts when purchased in bulk for premiums and
sales promotions as well as for fund-raising or educational use. Special editions or book excerpts
can also be created to specification. For details, contact the Special Sales Director at the address below.

Cover design by Paul Gamarello
Interior design by Barbara Balch
Cover photo by Penny De Los Santos

Workman Publishing Company, Inc.
708 Broadway
New York, NY 10003-9555
www.workman.com

Printed in the United States of America
First printing June 2003

10 9 8 7 6 5 4 3 2 1

Page xi. "To a Camper" by Mary S. Edgar, used by permission of John Gilchrist, executor of the estate of Mary S. Edgar. *Pages 15, 159, and 163.* Letters written by Marie Shufflebotham, Dorothy Bruegger Mausolff, and Peggy Holmes, respectively, reprinted from *Wohelo: Down Through the Years* by Charlotte Gulick Hewson, with permission of the author. *Pages 18–19 and 211.* "The Rites of Spring" and quote by Claudia Latimer Sullivan, respectively, reprinted from *Heartfelt: A Memoir of Camp Mystic Inspirations* by permission of the publisher, Eakin Press, Austin, TX. *Page 20.* "The Trip to Camp" by Ruth H. Blodgett and quote by Marion King Evans, reprinted from *Wyonegonic: The First Hundred Years* by Kendall Lione Gleason with permission of the publisher, Gleason Publishing Inc., Gwynn, VA. *Pages 30–31.* "Starting Fresh" by Judy Page Horton reprinted from *Camping Magazine* by permission of the American Camping Association, Inc.; © 2000 by the American Camping Association, Inc. *Page 44.* *The Other Side* memoir by Laura Shaine Cunningham reprinted from *A Place in the Country,* published by Riverhead Books, New York, NY. *Pages 51–52.* "How to Play Jacks" reprinted from *The Jacks Book* by Sally Chabert, published by Workman Publishing, New York, NY. *Page 63.* "A Place of Their Own" by Heather Brown Holleman reprinted with permission of the author. *Page 75.* "Prayer of a Sportsman" by Berton Braley reprinted with permission of his estate. *Page 80.* "The Warmth of Icy Waters" © Helen Schary Motro. *Page 94.* Popsicle Treasure Box instructions adapted from kinder-planet.com. *Pages ii, 117, 187, 199 and 211.* Quote from Demi Lockett Prentis, letter written by Pam Perry Walton and quotes by Martha Maynard and Claudia Latimer Sullivan, respectively, reprinted from *Summer Come, Summer Go: A Collection of Memories,* compiled by permission of Claudia Sullivan and published by Nortex Press, Austin, TX. *Page 146.* "What's the Story with Saltpeter" © 1994 Chicago Reader, Inc. Reprinted with permission. "The Straight Dope by Cecil Adams" is a registered trademark of the Chicago Reader, Inc. *Page 166.* Waldemar Creed, written by Sue Van Noy Willett and Carlyn Carmichael Wheat. Quoted in *The Waldemar Story: Camping in the Texas Hill Country,* compiled by Marsha English Elmore and published by Eakin Press, Austin, TX. *Pages 188–192.* "The Girls of Camp Lenore" © Diana Trilling; reprinted with permission of The Wylie Agency, Inc. All Girl Scout camp photographs reprinted by permission of Girl Scouts of the U.S.A.

WALDEMAR

TAPAWINGO

ROGINDEL

For Nancy Purcell

The camper whose name appears on this certificate has completed the following skills:

1. Double-hand spin
2. Cartwheel (front and side)
3. Finger twirl
4. Palm spin balance
5. Airplane series
6. One style strut
7. Beginning Leaps

CAMP KEAR-SARGE
Elkins, N. H.

MARIMETA

TO A CAMPER

You may think, my dear, when you grow quite old
You have left camp days behind,
But I know the scent of wood smoke
Will always call to mind
Little paths at twilight
And trails you used to find.

You may think someday you are quite grown up
And feel so worldly wise,
But suddenly from out of the past
A vision will arise
Of merry folk with brown bare knees
And laughter in their eyes.

You may live in a house, built to your taste
In the nicest part of town,
But someday for your old camp togs
You'd change your latest gown
And trade it for a balsam bed
Where stars all night look down.

You may find yourself grown wealthy
Have all that gold could buy
But you'd toss aside a fortune
For days 'neath an open sky
With sunlight on blue waters
And white clouds floating high.

For once you have been a camper
Then something has come to stay
Deep in your heart forever
Which nothing can take away
And heaven can only be heaven
With a camp in which to play.

—*Mary S. Edgar*

KICKAPOO KAMP

CONTENTS

"A few of us always compared anything good to: 'Isn't it just like camp?' When we first got married, we asked each other, 'Was your honeymoon good?' 'Yeah. It was just like camp.'"

—Susan Moldof Goldman Rubin, *Kear-Sarge*, 1948–53

TAPAWINGO

THE GIRLS OF SUMMER

I will always be a sleepaway camper at heart. There wasn't one thing I liked best about my camp; what I liked best was that there *was* my camp. If I could have stayed for the rest of my life, I would have. Camp was all about freedom: being free of my parents and brother and hometown, being free to express myself through sports and music and adventure. But most of all, camp gave me the freedom to connect to myself and to other girls. Camp was the place where I was treated as an individual while belonging to a neighborhood of friends into which I was 100 percent integrated, 24/7. It was the annual two-month window in my adolescence—a place where I felt valued by a community of people who cared deeply for one another.

I know I'm not the only grown woman who still dreams she's at camp, or who gets misty at the memory

WALDEN

of the morning-after hoarseness that followed a rousing color-war sing. I'd yearned to start a conversation with other similarly obsessed women for years, but I didn't really put my mind to it until 1998, when I began work on a documentary about "the lost girls of Camp Kear-Sarge." These were the women with whom I'd spent nine summers, from 1957 to the mid-'60s, but with whom I'd been out of touch for twenty-eight years. Kear-Sarge, in the White Mountains of New Hampshire, had closed in the '70s, our beloved director had died, and no network remained to connect us. I searched for my former bunk-mates and friends on the Internet, asking one woman to tell another, and then traveled the country for a year and a half with a video cam. I managed to find almost seventy women who had attended Kear-Sarge between 1933 and 1970, and each spoke with passion about the deep and enduring influence of her camp summers. To a woman, they remembered Kear-Sarge as the only place, geographically and emotionally, where they felt in touch with their authentic selves. The sanctuary of an all-girls environment was clearly a powerful antidote to the narrowness of what was expected of them as girls in what they called their "real life." Like me, they remembered that the success they experienced each year at camp fueled them for the ten months they were home.

GIRLS VACATION FUND CAMP

My documentary was the springboard for this book, an oral and visual affirmation of the effect of summers spent at girls' camps all over America, not just in New Hampshire. Now understand, an all-girls camp, whether it boasts a hundred or two hundred campers, is a plucky venture. Girls from different backgrounds, personalities still in flux, come together for a marathon of togetherness. *Sleepaway,* full of the voices and pictures of women who have attended these camps since their beginning a century ago, is a celebration of all these grand experiments in spunkiness. In this book, at least metaphorically, are the stories of thousands upon thousands of girls who discovered essential truths about themselves and others in the isolated community of camp.

When the first all-girls camp opened in Maine in 1902, camping was considered inappropriate for well-brought-up girls. Indeed, when camp pioneer Laura Mattoon, a teacher in a New York City private school, opened Camp Kehonka in Wolfeboro, New Hampshire, that same year, she scandalized many by permitting the girls to run around in bloomers in broad daylight. But still, within a decade or two, thousands of city-pale teenagers and young women were being sent to camps to refresh and strengthen themselves in the outdoors while enjoying the creative arts.

These early camps were laboratories for a passionate group of men and women, mostly educators in the Northeast, who envisioned that a love of nature and simplicity, as well as the values of loyalty, integrity, and respect, would be more easily inculcated in a beautiful environment where time was marked by sparkling mornings and lovelier sunsets. Determined to make their dreams real, these camp pioneers looked at first to the mountains and lakes of New England and the Adirondacks, perfect backdrops for the Keatsian romance they imagined developing between camper and environment. Before long, however, other camp leaders were turning their vision south and west so that children everywhere could experience the magic that was camp. Their vision caught on. By the 1930s and '40s, more and more parents were sending their daughters to camp so they could be "with nature" and away from the heat and disease of urban summers.

🌿

As I started this project, I fancied myself a social historian who would chronicle the memories that grassy fields, sandy shorelines, and piney breezes held for generations of women who had been campers before 1970. I was curious about the adventures of those girls of the early decades of the century, now great-grandmothers, who had worn burdensome woolen bloomers and high button boots to play basketball. I wanted to know how my own camp particulars resembled theirs, and if they and the other women I would talk to cherished camp as I did. I wondered if other women remembered camp as a series of moments that had created the person they had become. Was the vitality of girl-to-girl connection—the essence of my camp experience—still as alive for them? Was I the only one who could still relive the heart-wrenching sadness and grief of parting?

I have to admit, however, that I had zero curiosity about the experiences of post-1970 campers. Even though I had smoked cigarettes and rebelled against my parents' values in all sorts of ways (after all, I had spent four years at the University of Wisconsin in the sixties), I assumed that the campers of the last thirty years had corrupted my wonderland, substituting sex, drugs, and rock and roll for our more innocent raids on the kitchen and extravagant toilet-paper wrappings. But I soon realized that I had made a terrific mistake. The earliest photos in the camp archives looked remarkably like the most recent; wardrobe and hairstyles had changed, but these deliciously amateurish photos confirmed our cosmic oneness. Creating strong, competent, resilient girls has always been the goal of camp. It was weird, but I had to acknowledge that camp had gone on without me.

"Looking out over the lake, I felt enveloped in the most peaceful, loving utopia."

—Lynn Cohodus Stahl, *Nicolet*, 1953–59, 1961

WYONEGONIC

I now believe that a tangible spirit surrounds girls' camps today as surely as it did thirty and seventy-five and a hundred years ago: a spirit of friendship, loyalty that eclipses personal considerations, plus an appreciation of the simplicity often missing from campers' rest-of-the-year lives. It's a spirit that develops the best in us, that opens us up to new thoughts, new ideologies, new decisions. Looking back on my entire adolescence, I cannot remember my mother telling me anything I hadn't already learned at camp—ever! If I wanted to know something, the other girls knew it. If they didn't know it, they made it up. I think that explains why, when Rhoda Booth scheduled a reunion in 1982—fourteen years after my last summer— her invitation sent me over the moon with anticipation. My friends thought I was some kind of lunatic as I counted the days. "It's *camp* you're talking about. This isn't how we know you. Grow up." They couldn't understand. But I think almost every girl who ever went to camp will. They know, as I do, that it *is* possible—and eminently worthwhile and pleasurable—to recapture the days of youth. It's really not that hard. All you have to do is refuse to close the camp book. I haven't. Why should I? And why should anyone?

Laurie Susan Kahn
Noyac, New York, January 2003

GIRLS VACATION FUND CAMP

EARLY GIRLS' CAMPS

1902
Kehonka
Pinelands
Wyonegonic

1903
Barnard

1904
Quanset

1905
Aloha
Susquebannocks

1906
Farwell

1907
Alford Lake
Moy-Mo-Da-Yo
Runoia
Wohelo Luther
Gulick Camps

1908
Hanoum
Oneka

1910
Wawnock

1911
Greystone
Michigamee
Tripp Lake
Acconac
Quinibeck
Sandstone

1912
Minnewawa
Arey
Songo

1914
Holiday Camps
Rocky Mountain
Dancing Camp
Kawajiwin (now
Kamaji)
Kechuwa
Arbutus
Newfound

1915
Tall Pines
Pinewood
Aloha Hive

1916
Arcadia
Keystone
Walden
Chunn's Cove
Junaluska
Meenahga
Lochearn

1917
Idylewyld
Wabanaki
Perry-Mansfield
Camps
Pinecliffe

1918
Willapa
Kinnikinnik
Bryn Afon

ALOHA

TRIPP LAKE

Chapter 1

AND AWAY WE GO

In the mid-1950s my father discovered that his best friend from camp, John Bateman, owned Camp Sunapee, a boys' camp in New London, New Hampshire; at that moment, my brother's summer fate was sealed. It made sense to choose a camp for me nearby. That's how I ended up meeting Rhoda and Lee Booth, the owners of Camp Kear-Sarge, one Sunday afternoon in January of 1956. They came to our house with a slide show. I was smitten and that was that.

When my parents signed me up for camp, I assumed they were shipping me off to give themselves a vacation from parenthood. I imagined they would spend the summer dancing around the house, acting silly. But from the

WALDEN

moment I arrived at Kear-Sarge, I couldn't have cared less about their reason for sending me, nor did I give a moment's thought to what they might be doing. At sleepaway camp, I felt I had come home. I was a million miles from homesick. I never wanted any other kids from my hometown on Long Island to come with me to camp. It was my special place, separated from the "real world" by a line both imaginary and vivid.

Every June, New York City's Grand Central Station was the site of a thousand good-byes as campers, armed with suitcases, cameras, tennis rackets, and stuffed animals, gathered to begin the trek to New England and the Adirondacks. Each camp had an assigned car or two, which meant that for several days in late June conductors were driven crazy as hordes of eager, wound-up, giggling campers bounced from car to car. There were card games to play, movie magazines and comics to read, but few of us were able to concentrate. We were on the glory road.

When we reached our station, a phalanx of buses, pickup trucks, and station wagons would be loaded with singing girls, all the old-timers looking out for landmarks on the final phase of the journey. When I was young, I thought this ritual belonged only to me and my friends. I now know it was repeated all over the country year after year, decade after decade. And so it continues to this day.

UNIDENTIFIED

"The whole year, no matter what went wrong, I knew everything would be okay once I got to camp." —Toby Boyer Freeman, *Mataponi, 1962–72*

GIRL SCOUT CAMP

FIRST-TIMERS' FEARS

I'll hate it.

They'll lose my trunk and duffel bag, and I'll have to wear the same outfit for eight weeks.

I'll get the worst counselor.

No one will like me.

No one else will still be wearing an undershirt.

No one else will be wearing a bra.

I'll be homesick and cry a lot.

They'll make me put my face in the lake.

My parents will move while I'm away.

Everyone else will already have friends there.

I will hate my parents forever for making me go.

Someone will tell me what to do every minute of the day.

GIRLS VACATION FUND CAMP

WYONEGONIC

LETTERS HOME

Wohelo, 1916

Sweet Mother:
First of all I must tell you how I prize your letter that greeted me when I arrived—this very evening. To have you for my friend makes me more sure of all the many things I don't understand but hope for—of hidden beauties, eternal love and divine sympathy. There wells up in my heart at this moment a deep, silent desire to prove worthy, never to falter but to be strong, helpful and loving always. Thank you, precious lady, for your interest and friendship.

I left Great Spruce Head early this morning directly after breakfast, which was at 7:30 Island time (6:30 Eastern time). . . . "The Porter boat"—no, it was Capt. Green's "Evelyn"—took me to Dark Harbor, Nancy bearing me company thus far. From Dark Harbor on Islesborough I took the "Sierra de Monto" to Rockland, thence to Portland by train, on to Sebago Lake. On the Sebago Lake train there was the Boston group of campers, which was by far

the smaller group. The New York party had preceded us in the morning. At Sebago Lake Station we were met by "Tiddy," a very efficient, sunny young woman who took charge of our trunk check and towed us to camp. We came on an evidently public boat and over rather rough water. Finally many sought refuge in the cabin, where there was a general toss and catch of personal equations. Overhead the weather was suspicious, marvelously so. We reached Wohelo at 4:30, I think. Camp is wonderful, wonderful, unspeakably wonderful! I am happy here already. There is abroad everywhere the spirit of good fellowship.

—Marie Shufflebotham

"**We met at the Jacksonville station between 7:30 and 8:30 P.M.** The train didn't leave until 9:00, but we got on about 8:30. Our car was a very busy place with all the mothers and fathers saying good-bye to the girls. The coach was busy the rest of the night with the running up and down the aisles and swinging from the upper berths. There was much confusion with girls losing their bubble gum, candy, purses, and hats.

It was past midnight when we finally settled down. Then some girls in the lower two berths woke us all up complaining about sleeping on chicken bones, which they had eaten earlier. They finally got all the bones out of the bed and we all tried to sleep again.

This time we were more successful, and soon this hard night of snatching covers was over. We all got up early and waited at least an hour for the diner to open, then waited another hour in line. After we had all eaten, we spent the

WINNISQUAM

next impatient hours sitting on a mountainside while another train engine came to take us to Hendersonville. There we were met by a bus and taken to camp."

— Claire Chestnut, *Keystone, 1941–46, 1949*

GIRL SCOUT CAMP

"**When the camp materials would arrive,**
I would go completely haywire until we had mailed them
in. Since it wasn't always clear that we would have enough
money to afford camp, I took responsibility for contributing
myself. At age eleven, I saved every penny I earned and
was given and contributed almost $400 (or about a third)
to my camp fees."

—Juliane Eberhard, *Glen Bernard, 1982–89*

CAMP NAKANAWA MISSION STATEMENT

THE PURPOSE OF CAMP LIFE IS THREEFOLD: FIRST, TO GIVE
ENJOYMENT THROUGH GAMES, SPORTS, AMUSEMENTS, DIVER-
SIONS OF VARIOUS SORTS, WITH A VIEW TO TONING AND BRAC-
ING THE WHOLE SYSTEM AND THEREBY MAKING LIFE FOR EACH
GIRL MORE WORTHWHILE; SECOND, TO ENABLE THOSE DESIRING
IT THE PRIVILEGE OF RETRIEVING ACADEMIC FAILURES DUE TO
ILLNESS, ETC., AND OF TAKING ADVANCED WORK; THIRD, TO
TEACH THE ART OF GENUINE COMPANIONSHIP, AN ART CALLING
FOR THE GRACES OF PATIENCE, COURTESY, CONSIDERATION,
KINDLINESS.

WYONEGONIC

The Rites of Spring

"Growing up in Fort Worth, I knew it was summer when I began to pack my trunk for summer camp. One day, usually in mid-March, I would begin to rummage through last year's clothes searching for my favorite pair of shorts and a much-loved soft and faded T-shirt. Each year I set up my trunk at the end of the hall that divided my parents' bedroom from the guest room. I wore a path from my room to the guest room to the place at the end of the hall, collecting necessities and sorting clothes for camp. This was my annual ritual, my rite of spring.

I did not approach my first summer at camp with such excitement. . . .

From my journal, 1964:
I knew no one. I didn't know any of the cute songs they sang and I didn't understand any of the secret phrases they uttered. . . . I feel out, alone, rejected even before I begin. . . .

The bus is filled with roaring, chanting, singing (if you can call it that), and the bus driver must be going crazy. By the time we passed Austin the singing of camp songs had reached a fevered pitch. Each time we pass some landmark that the girls recognize, an even louder roar goes up. . . . By now everyone is singing, laughing, pointing, screaming, bobbing up and down in their seats . . . all except me. . . . 'I'm so afraid I will be unhappy,' I think to myself. Suddenly a hush comes over the bus. Everyone sits down and begins to crane their necks in the most peculiar way. The only sound is the sucking noise made by shoes moving up and down on the sticky floor, and the whine of the bus engine. Everyone is looking for some-thing. 'What are they looking for . . . what does everyone see?' I ask the question out loud because I want to see also.

Immediately the girl sitting next to me squeals, 'THERE it is.'. . .

Well, it might as well have been a holy vision and I still couldn't see it. The sunlight was so fierce that I couldn't see anything outside the bus window, except the river and the looming hills that walled the road. 'No, wait a minute,' I thought. 'I do see something . . . it's . . . it's the word M Y S T I C spelled out on top of the hill to our left. So that's it?' I felt pleased that finally I knew what all the commotion was about. Now I had something I could relate to. Just as I was settling in to the idea that I might like this place, everyone began pulling belongings out of the overhead racks, from under the seats, and from anywhere anything was stored away. It resembled 'abandon ship.' No one seemed to care if they were getting their own things, they were just tugging and ripping anything they could get their hands on. And the chaperone began again her pleas of 'Girls . . . girls . . . ladies . . .' And to no avail.

From the midst of arms flailing, duffel bags flying through air, and general pandemonium I saw the river at Mystic. It took my breath away. . . . From somewhere deep inside me I began to move. I too began to grab for my pillow, my fan, anything I could get my hands on. I may not have been sure about camp, I may have had feelings of regret at being there, but one thing I did know . . . I was not going to be left behind. . . .

That was my introduction to Camp Mystic. Shortly after I was escorted to my cabin, Seventh Heaven, I met my first friend, also a first-timer. By dinnertime that night, I was hooked. I loved camp. I loved everything about it; the tribes, the games, the classes, even the heat and mosquitoes and naptime—I loved all of it."

—Claudia Latimer Sullivan, *Mystic, 1964–79*

WYONEGONIC

The Trip to Camp

Into the great North Station
   we walked,
My little cousin and I.
Fast and furiously we talked
Of things that had gone by.

But soon we saw a motley throng
Of girls, all going to camp;
Bidding farewell with faces long
And handkerchiefs all damp.

Some with paddles and others
   with bows,
While all had dress-suit cases
Which stood in rows and rows
   and rows
In a million different places.

They all at last climbed into
   the car
And one fond brother cried:
"Don't lose your trunk-key,
   Lydia!"
The girls looked mortified.

At Wyonegonic they were going
   to stay
And for the long ride settled
   down.
But when ice-cream appeared
   their way
They got up and rushed around.

At Brownfield station we got
   out
For a Denmark bus to wait.
And some began to make a fuss
For it was getting late.

At Denmark Inn we met Miss
   Giles
And Mr. and Mrs. Cobb.
Being told we were going to
   camp, two miles,
Into canoes got the mob.

Winding down the lake we
   went
Towed by a motorboat.
Till we caught the sight of some
   brown tents
And of a few girls took note.

At last all have come to their
   destination
And each to her tent makes way,
Where she begins to make
   preparations
For a summer full of play.

—Ruth H. Blodgett,
Wyonegonic Camp Log, 1912

"I graduated from school and went to brand-new Camp Wyonegonic. We were the first girls' camp in New England, and we were a novelty to the people around us. Hiking one day, we asked a farmer the best way to get back to camp. He told us, and then added: 'You'll never make it.' How little did he know."

—**Marion King Evans,** *Wyonegonic, 1902*

"Camp was my heaven and my escape."
—Susan Rifkin Karon, *Matoaka*, 1969–79

WYONEGONIC

CAMP COSTUME

Keystone Camp for Girls 1920

A uniform camp costume is required because it adds not only much to the neat appearance of camp, but to a feeling of comradeship and unity among all campers and counselors. Except for plays, fancy dress parties, church, and some trips, the wearing of the regular camp costume is compulsory for both campers and counselors.

The required articles are:
8 or more white middies
1 pair navy blue serge bloomers
3 or more navy blue cotton bloomers
2 navy blue middy ties (half square)
1 heavy sweater (navy blue or tan preferred)
2 pair high sneakers (white or brown)
Stockings—tan cotton or wool
1 pair hiking shoes with strong soles and
    low heels (moccasin type preferred)
2 woolen bathing suits
2 bathing caps
1 rain coat
1 bath robe and slippers
Blue duck hat
1 pillow and 3 pillow cases
3 single sheets
2 pairs dark woolen blankets
2 laundry bags
Towels, wash rags, underwear,
    handkerchiefs, and all necessary toilet
    articles for eight weeks.

Desirable things to bring are: flashlight, poncho, canteen, kodak, tennis racquet and ball, musical instruments, riding habit, costumes for plays, games, worthwhile books as a contribution to the camp library.

Jewelry and all superfluous articles should be left at home as there is no place for them in the orderliness and simplicity of camp life.

"It was the only place I wasn't anyone's sister or daughter. I was just me."—Abby Kirschner, *Glenmere, 1964–66*

KEYSTONE

OUTFIT AND PROGRAM INFORMATION

Oneka 2002

Greetings to all Oneka campers! We are happy to have you with us for the 2002 season. Below is our list of articles that you should bring to camp:

Clothing

6–8 pairs red shorts
Supply of shorts
8–10 white shirts
Supply of T-shirts
1 RED swimsuit (one-piece)
2 extra swimsuits (one-piece)
2 WHITE swimcaps
15 pair sport socks
15 pair underpants
1 RED sweater/sweatshirt
Several sweatshirts or sweaters
3 pairs jeans
Several warm PJ's
Warm bathrobe (*optional*)
Warm jacket (*optional*)
Raincoat or poncho
2 pairs sneakers
Flip-flops or water sandals
Duck shoes or rain boots
1 laundry bag
1 trunk (footlocker)

Bedding & Towels

3–4 warm blankets
2 sets single or cot size sheets
3 pillow cases
1 pillow
6–8 towels (bath or swim)
2 face cloths
Outdoor sleeping bag
Mosquito net for bed (*optional*)
  (*Seniors and Ints. only*)

Miscellaneous

1 mess kit
Knife, fork, spoon
1 plastic cup
1 refillable water bottle
Flashlight and batteries
Tennis racquet & 1 can tennis
  balls
1 pair shin guards
2 molded mouth guards
  (*Seniors and Ints. only*)
Writing paper and stamps
Camera and film
Toiletries
Shower bucket or
  carryall
Insect repellent (*optional*)
Masquerade costume
  (*Juniors only*)
Sunscreen or
  lotion
Swim goggles
  (*optional*)

For the benefit of new campers, we wear red shorts and white shirts for supper each evening, for Sundays, for campfires and special events. Most of the white shirts that you bring should be plain or "Oneka" logo shirts, though white shirts with small pictures or writing can be worn to supper. For normal daily activities, shirts and shorts of any color are fine.

Campers keep most of their clothing in their trunks. In Junior and Int. rows, sheets, towels, etc., are kept on shelves. In Senior row plastic crates can be used for storage, but they are impractical for Junior and Int. rows.

TAPAWINGO

My First Summer at a Minnesota Camp

Written at age eleven after a memorable eight weeks

"Mother was very much interested in finding a camp that I could go to during the summer. She said that she had found a camp for my sister, but not for me. One evening we visited some friends. They have four children, two girls and two boys. Our friends had had company for dinner and talked about camps in Minnesota. Mother asked me if I wanted to go so far away from home. I told her I didn't care how far away from home I went as long as it was a good camp.

Later that night Daddy and Mother talked over the things that had been said about camp and decided I could go to Minnesota. We had a great many things to get in order to have everything that was necessary. These are some of the things: 2 army blankets, 4 pair of blue shorts, 5 blue shirts, 1 white shirt, 1 pair of white shorts, 1 pair of corduroy knickers and overalls, if we wanted them. These were not all the things we had to have but some of the most important.

We left Tulsa June 25th at 12:30. Everybody who was going was saying goodbye because they were not going to see each other for about eight weeks. We went on the Santa Fe train. We had supper on the train and reached Kansas City, Missouri, about 7 o'clock Tuesday night. The Tulsa girls met the Oklahoma City and Ardmore girls in Kansas City about 8 o'clock. Their counselor was from Shawnee, Oklahoma. The train didn't leave Kansas City until 11:30 so the younger ones stayed in the station and shopped around and had a very good time. The older ones were taken to a picture show but they did not get to see all of it.

We younger ones were so tired that by 11 o'clock we were ready to get on the train and go to bed. Our chaperone took us to the train and let us get on. The older ones came in about twenty minutes later.

It was about a quarter to twelve when I asked the porter why we did not go. He told me that the engine was broken. When we did finally start, we were glad because it was so stuffy and the fresh air felt good. But the Kansas City girls did not settle down in bed until after 2:30. They had brought candy and two or three portable victrolas. They played these and ate candy until their counselor came and made them go to bed. They came down to our part of the car and got some of us up. We went down there and ate about two pieces of candy, and then we were so tired and sleepy that we said good night and went back to our berths in the other end of the car. The next night was more quiet, and everybody was certainly glad."

—**Carolyn Louise Barton,**
Kawajian (now Kamaji), 1929

KINIYA

WE-HA-KEE

"The height of fun was riding the Pullman train to Portland, Maine, with my sister; each of us had a shoebox full of special food treats to last us through the trip. We'd stay up all night going from car to car, meeting kids from the other camps. In the morning there was a box breakfast, which I remember clearly: a hard-boiled egg, Drake's Pound Cake, an orange, and a container of milk. When the bus met us at the train, we fought for the back row of seats, because the ride up and down those Maine hills was just like a roller coaster and the bumps were always best in the back."

—Peggy Weiner Smith, *Tapawingo, 1958–60*

ALOHA

PINECLIFFE

Camp Spirit—we have heard a great deal about it—we have been chided for not having it, we have been complimented when we exhibit it—it has carried us through many trying situations—that mysterious, intangible, and all-necessary something called "Camp Spirit."

What morale is to an army, Camp Spirit is to a camp, and when all else fails, Camp Spirit carries us through.

What is it? You know and I know. It's the thing which welds us all together, the feeling which makes us do disagreeable tasks when we'd like to grumble; it makes us take pride in our camp, and in our work and in our play; it makes us smile when cold, wet, and hungry; it carries us over the last mile and up the long hard climb and brings us home happy.

Camp Spirit is a thing which depends upon the leaders, for the great part, and its presence spells happiness. It grows around the campfire, as we sing our camp songs, as we swing along the road, shoulder to shoulder or as we work and play. You can tell it by the warm feeling around your heart. It's a dear, precious invaluable something, and if you have acquired it, you are leaving camp that much richer. You will take it home and develop it into school spirit and college spirit and civic spirit, and you will never again do things in the same old careless, irresponsible way.

Keystone Camp (1925)

"**The first day of my first summer at camp,** I watched as other campers arrived, screaming gleefully as they spotted and reunited with friends. One group wrapped their arms around one another's shoulders and broke into song; others just hugged and jumped up and down. At ten, I was stunned that girls who were not related could be that happy to see each other. Of course, for the next five summers I was one of those hugging, screaming, singing girls."

—Robin Dobson, *Tegawitha, 1955–60*

THE OTHER SIDE

"**At camp I learned how mean** girls can be to each other."

—Gerry Penn Wexler, *Matoaka, 1961–66*

GIRLS VACATION FUND CAMP

To make friendships which shall last through life. To develop strong healthy bodies through regular exercise, good food and rest in the pure mountain air. To create a love of God's out-of-doors and a reverence for His handiwork. To bring out the hidden possibilities which lie within each girl, and to help her "find herself."

"**I was nine years old my first summer at camp.** On the overnight train from Memphis to Chicago, I met several girls who were going to my camp. We spent time together as we waited for girls from other parts of the country to arrive, and while we walked around, one of the Memphis girls told me she was sure we'd be friends since we were both fat. At that moment we became best friends."

—Eileen Pachter Pink, *Nokomis, 1957–59*

ROBINDEL

WE WELCOME YOU

We welcome you to (*name of camp*);
We're mighty glad you're here.
We'll set the air reverberating
    with a mighty cheer.
We'll sing you in; we'll sing you
    out;
To you we'll raise a mighty
    shout.
Hail, hail, the gang's all here,
And we welcome you to (*name
    of camp*).

TALL GIRLS, SHORT GIRLS

Tall girls, short girls, fat or
    thin,
Whatcha gonna do when the
    heat sets in?
With nothing to do, nothing to
    say,
Now's the time to pack your
    bags and come away.

Come to (*name of camp*), where
    the breezes blow;
Come to (*name of camp*), where
    you swim and row.
Answer that ever-luring call;
Come to (*name of camp*), the best
    of all!

Starting Fresh

" **The year was 1951. I was six weeks shy of turning nine, and my father had just committed suicide. We lived in a west Texas town**

small enough for everyone to know our business. The times being what they were, nobody spoke directly to my brother or me about what had happened, but everyone knew and we knew they knew. Deep shame permeated our lives, and we lived pretty much holed up in our modest little frame house.

About a month after Daddy died, a catalog came in the mail from Camp Arrowhead, a girls' camp in the Texas hill country. Soon after, a letter arrived from my grandmother saying that if I wanted to go she would send me. I pored over the black-and-white pictures of happy girls paddling canoes and participating in Indian rituals. The cover was cleverly cut in the shape of an arrowhead, and each day I traced the outline with my fingers. I was not an adventurous child, but I was ready to sign on, and so the arrangements were made . . .

After a long journey in Grandmother's big humpbacked car, we arrived at camp amid a rush of cars from all over Texas and Louisiana—parents fretting and hugging, campers flying into one another's arms, counselors and staff herding groups of girls this way and that. I was terrified and exhausted. But most of all I felt I had been handed a new chance at life. Here nobody knew about my sick, crazy, dead father. Nobody knew the scandals that made up our life. For five and a half glorious weeks, I was free to be any me I wanted to be. Nobody knew my story, and more important, nobody really cared. In my cabin we were swept up in the drama of waiting to learn whether we newcomers would join the tribe of the Kickapoos or that of the Pawnees. I was pretty sure I wanted to be a Kickapoo, but the instant I pulled the paper

with a 'P' inscribed on it, I knew I'd been wrong all along. I was given a gold silk kerchief to wear with the regulation white camp shirt, and no knight of old was ever prouder of his colors.

I settled happily and easily into camp routine. I loved the comfort of the daily schedule—and marveled at so many things to learn and do. Marveled, too, to discover that I was good at a lot of them. I had a real flair for riflery, despite a lazy eye, and learned swim strokes that first summer. Camp was wonderful, with real college women as counselors and a terrific staff that could teach you anything you wanted to learn. I was treated with respect and learned the joy of

GLEN MOHR

First Evening.

ALOHA

living in a community of shared values. In my favorite class, an exceptionally talented choral director whipped the Pawnee Pipers and the Kickapoo Chorus into shape for the final concert.

I attended Arrowhead for five summers in a row. Each summer was the annual highlight of my young life, and the lessons I learned there were invaluable— lessons in trust, sportsmanship, pride of accomplishment and friendship.

When I was forty-two, my husband and I were graced with a beautiful baby girl, who has Down's syndrome. We knew we could provide for our daughter's physical needs, but we wanted so much more for her than that. We wanted a place where she and others like her could feel safe and accepted yet still meet new challenges.

And so we founded Down Home Ranch. For many of our campers, as for me a half-century ago, camp is the highlight of their year. For too many, their lives have been defined by what they *can't* do, and huge amounts of energy have been devoted to compensating. At camp, however, they discover the thrill of accomplishing those things that matter to *them*. (Maybe the world doesn't recognize the importance of learning the silly song we sing to our cooks, but trust me, the world is wrong.)

When camp opens each year, and the first returning camper bolts from the car to give me a gigantic bear hug, my heart goes back to Camp Arrowhead, still nestled on the banks of the Guadalupe River. Several years ago I drove out there, expecting to find it smaller and diminished—the way most things are that we remember being grand as a child. But it remains as beautiful as ever. And I've learned by experience that beautiful, grand places don't just happen. They are created by people with vision, who have love and respect for what they are doing and for those they serve. A good thing done well is a glory to God."

— Judy Page Horton,
Arrowhead, 1951–55

PINECLIFFE

"**I was five years old.** I lived with my parents and baby sister in a bucolic Massachusetts town. Every day I'd ride my bicycle or walk to the beach some blocks away. Then, one hot day in June, my parents scheduled a car trip to New York to visit my grandparents. On day two of our visit, we got up early and drove to Grand Central Station, where my parents introduced me to a girl who I thought was at least my mother's age, but who, in fact, was probably sixteen or seventeen. Her name was Roberta Levenson; they said she would be my train counselor. I knew what a train was, so I wasn't afraid of that. But I didn't know what a counselor was, and no one explained. And then my parents basically ran away. I can't imagine what they were thinking. Maybe they thought I'd resist leaving them for the summer. They'd have been wrong."

— Marcelle Harrison, *Kear-Sarge, 1947–59*

KAMAJI MOTTO

Daughters grow up just once.

Chapter 2

CUBBIES, COUNSELORS & BM CHARTS

I had two major surprises my first night at Kear-Sarge. There I was in Bunk 11, a cabin with windows that had only screens, raw pine walls covered with shoe polish signatures of previous tenants, and not an iota of privacy. I was in the midst of seven strangers and yet expected to change into my pajamas. As a nine-year-old I wasn't unduly modest or self-conscious, but I couldn't believe that my bunk had no changing room or closet in which I could hide. There were only tall crates called cubbies, in which we kept all our stuff, and I couldn't fit in there. Exactly how I navigated putting on my PJs that night, or my shorts or a bathing suit later that week, has fallen out of my knapsack of memory. But

BERNADETTE

I do know that within a couple of days I was cavorting around the bunk with or without clothes, skinny-dipping before breakfast, and running to the clothesline nude to fetch a bathing suit. Being naked became incidental to being together.

The other wonder of that first night was my introduction to the BM chart, an oak-tag form taped to the inside of our toilet stall door. Our last names had been alphabetized and color-coded on the left side, with rows of boxes signifying the days of the week. Our junior counselor casually explained that each time we had a bowel movement we were to place a check mark next to our name. At the end of each week we could look forward to reviewing our chart with the camp nurse. For my first three summers not a day went by that my bathroom behavior wasn't monitored, and then, without explanation, the charts disappeared.

Bunk living gave me the opportunity to create and be part of a community. It taught me to share not only clothes and tennis rackets, but also feelings. In the give-and-take of camp life, with its intimate contacts, I learned what was acceptable, what the social boundaries were and how to harmonize with camp customs. I found the best side of me at camp, especially with my bunk-mates. There was no such thing as a bad day; I was never

TAPAWINGO

moody or miserable. I was cheerful and helpful, willing to try anything and to trust my interior landscape. I learned I had the seeds inside me to be a confident, competent person, and I was able to be that person for eight weeks every year. I knew how much I loved camp when I realized I could have as much fun on a rainy day as I did on any other.

And counselors—older, more competent versions of us—were a big part of the whole happy gestalt. They were encouraging and nurturing and so different from our teachers, who were older and too much like our parents.

GIRLS VACATION FUND CAMP

On that rare occasion when we'd hear or see a counselor being scolded, it made her more like us: the imperfect victim of insensitive and overbearing adults. Counselors were our pals, even as they were role models. We worshiped them as paragons of what we could aim for—strength, competency, resiliency.

But more to the point, they were completely and utterly focused on us. Maybe they were thinking about their night off, but we felt we had them all to ourselves. They never worried if they "looked fat." They never changed a bathing suit before heading to the waterfront because some guy would be there. They taught us kindness and caring, and encouraged our efforts. They were our confidantes. We could ask them questions, express our concerns, and admit our confusion. Within this summer family, this cocoon of friendship, we could be happy and secure.

Like many of the women I've spoken with about camp, I've never again been in a circumstance that was as consistently connected. I went to college hoping to find something approximating camp and was frustrated when I didn't. But sometimes now, when I'm sitting around with a bunch of women getting real loose, just relaxing, there are moments when I can feel it, and that's when I think, "*This* is what camp was like."

ILLAHEE

THE SOUND OF FOUR HANDS CLAPPING

A SAILOR WENT TO SEA, YOU SEE

(Clapping pattern: clap own hands; clap both hands against partner's hands; clap own hands; clap partner's right hand with yours; clap own hands; clap partner's left hand with yours. Repeat sequence.)

A sailor went to sea, you see,
To see what he could see, you see.
But all that he could see, you see,
Was the bottom of the deep blue
    sea sea sea.

Oh, Helen had a steamboat;
The steamboat had a bell.
When Helen went to heaven,
The steamboat went to . . .

Hello, operator,
Just give me number nine.
If the line is busy,
I'll kick your big . . .

Behind the old piano
There was a piece of glass.
Helen slipped upon it
And hurt her little . . .

Ask me for a muffin,
I'll give you some old bread.
And if you do not like it
Just go and soak your head.

I AM A PRETTY LITTLE DUTCH GIRL

(Clapping pattern: clap own hands; clap partner's right hand with yours; clap own hands; clap partner's left hand with yours; clap both hands against partner's hands; clap own shoulders; clap own knees. Repeat sequence.)

I am a pretty little Dutch girl,
As pretty as pretty can be.
And all the boys in the neigh-
    borhood
Go crazy over me.

My boyfriend's name is Fatty;
He comes from Cincinnati
With a pimple on his nose
And three green toes.
And this is how my story goes.

I L-O-V-E, love you,
All the T-I-M-E, time.
I K-I-S-S, kiss you,
Please be M-I-N-E,
Mine, mine, mine.

ILLAHEE

ALOHA HIVE

Taking the following steps should keep you out of trouble when the counselor comes by to inspect the quality of your bed-making skills:

1. Assuming that you're not using a fitted sheet, begin making your bed by draping the bottom sheet on the mattress and tucking it in at the foot and head of the bed. Make hospital corners at both ends.

HOW TO MAKE A HOSPITAL CORNER.

Standing on one side of the bed, pull up the free edge of the bottom sheet about fifteen inches from the end of the bed. Lift it up so it makes a diagonal fold. Lay the fold on the mattress. Take the part of the sheet that is hanging and tuck it under the mattress. Drop the fold and pull it smooth, then tuck it under the mattress.

2. Tuck sides in tightly.

3. Drape the top sheet over the bed, being sure to bring the hemmed end of the sheet just up to the head of the bed.

4. Carefully drape the blanket on top of the sheet, being careful not to wrinkle it. (Tip: Mark the center of the blanket with a small X so it's easier to center it on the sheet.) The top of the blanket should come to about a foot below the headboard.

5. Make hospital corners on both sides of the bed, tucking in top sheet and blanket simultaneously.

6. Fold the top sheet over the blanket.

7. Position the pillow at the head of the bed.

8. Tuck in both sides, pulling as tightly as you can.

9. Bounce a quarter on the bed. If it doesn't bounce, your bed is not tightly enough made. Keep tugging and tucking until the quarter bounces, or start over.

10. DO NOT SIT ON YOUR BED UNTIL AFTER INSPECTION!

GIRL SCOUT CAMP

"**Everybody dreaded the day** it was their turn to clean the john. My favorite thing on the job wheel was sweeping, so I would beg the other girls to trade jobs with me. They'd run away whenever they saw me coming."

—Stacey Green, *Raquette Lake, 1983–86*

GIRL SCOUT CAMP

"**At home I had no chores.** We lived in a small apartment, which was always a big mess. Beds were not made; dishes were still on the table or in the sink. Life was very different at camp. I learned about a personal discipline, a sense of self, and that there were ways of doing things other than my family's style. I liked not feeling lazy; I liked being neat. Most of all, I noticed other people's reactions to me. They expected more of me than my parents did, and I was able to meet their expectations. I thrived on the challenge."

—Bernice Haase Luck,
Beverly, 1942–45

41

WYONEGONIC

HA-HA-HA-HA-HA!

This is how to play Ha-Ha! (as if anyone could ever forget):

One girl lies on the bunk floor. The next girl lies down and puts her head on the stomach of the girl ahead of her. Continue in this fashion until every girl in the bunk is on the floor. The first girl says, "Ha!" The next girl says, "Ha-ha!" The third girl says, "Ha-ha-ha!" and so on.

The object of the game is to NOT burst out laughing, which is impossible.

"Poor Suzie's sheath knife fell off her belt in the outhouse and she had to reach down to retrieve it!"

—Barbara Rioux Novak,
Sherwood, 1942–48

WALDEN

"In the weeks following the loss of my mother, a turn of fate sent me north to true country for the first time. It was decided two weeks

after her death that I should join my friend and neighbor Susan at the camp where she had just started the season. I had campaigned to join her—more than campaigned, I had begged and threatened in the relentless way of an eight-year-old—until one morning I found myself headed for camp on an ancient bus that seemed to sputter exhaust at the thought of climbing the mountainous road to Upper Cragsdale. What I saw should have warned me: the camp was situated on a slope so steep that it seemed as if the bunkhouses could slide down the mountain. Everything listed to the left, including the Camp Ava sign. This tilt reflected the camp politics—it had been founded by socialist labor union leaders. At the height of the season, the place appeared abandoned. Even the crabgrass had died. The center field was denuded.

The advertised swimming pool turned out to be a slime pit, dammed by concrete, that leached turquoise paint chips.

I could not grasp that this was the real Camp Ava. I had envisioned the camp so completely that I was certain that my notion of it had to exist somewhere—maybe on the other side of the mountain. The weeks that followed were an encapsulated version of my future country experiences: I went into 'nature shock'—stung by bugs, inflamed by rashes, and more susceptible to fear than delight when I found myself alone in the longed-for wilderness. But I would also find what I sought— solace in a sylvan setting. I had arrived a week late in a ten-week session—I might as well have arrived in the next century. In the abbreviated social time span, the week I missed could never be made up. Friendships had

formed, rivalries flared. Bunks were divided, and the bunk wars had begun.

Camp Ava had advertised swimming, nature hikes, and horseback riding, but the actual activities at camp were diarrhea . . . and attempted escape. During my nine-week stay, I would experience most of the highlights, with a few personal detours."

—Laura Shaine Cunningham, *"Ava,"* 1955

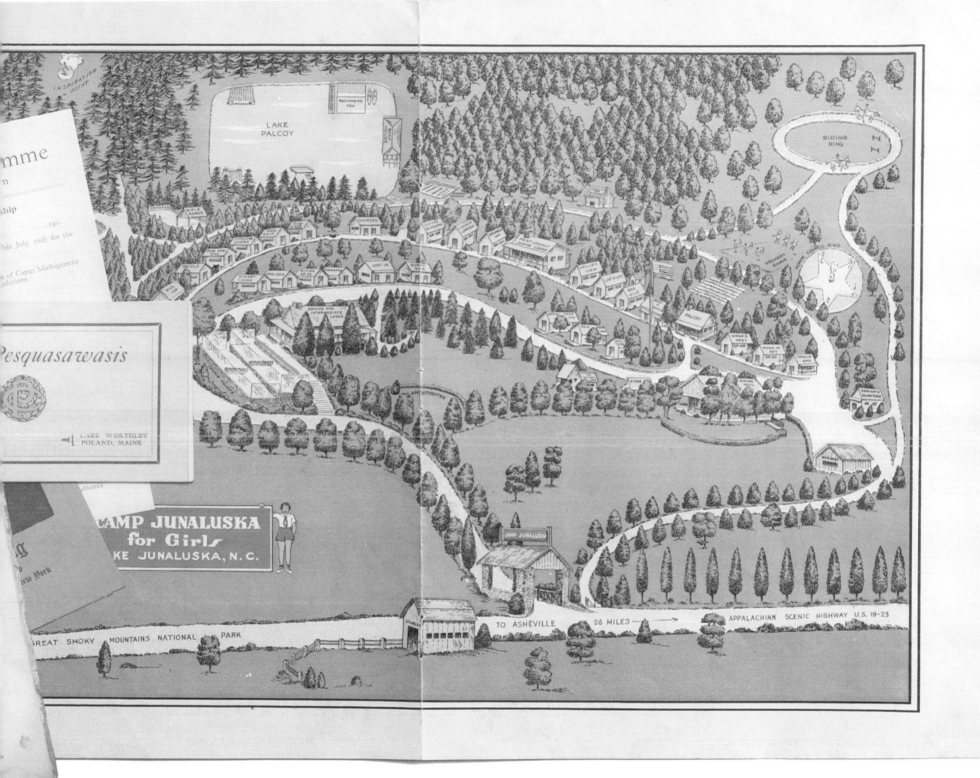

(Sing the song all the way through with hand gestures. Next time through, hum the first line but keep using gestures throughout. The next time through, you'll be humming the first two lines, repeating in that manner until the entire song is hummed—but always acted out.)

In a cabin in the woods *(make out-line of house with index fingers)*,

Little man by the window stood *(place hand above eyes, as if searching the landscape)*,

Saw a rabbit hopping by *(point index and middle fingers up to represent the bunny's ears and bounce hand up and down hop-ping motion)*,

Knocking at his door *(pretend to knock with fist)*.

"Help me! *(throw hands up in air)* Help me! *(again)* Help!" *(and again)* he cried,

"'Fore the hunter shoots me dead." *(pretend to take aim with index finger as rifle)*

"Little rabbit come inside *(make welcoming gesture to motion 'come here')*,

"Safely you'll abide" *(make bunny's ears with right hand and hug and pet rabbit with left hand)*.

NORTHWAY LODGE

CAMP KAMAJI OBJECTIVES FOR CAMPERS

To develop responsibility for achieving one's potential

To express a concern for others

Decision-making

To develop perspective

To persevere

To delay gratification

To live independently but with community awareness

To be able to assess risks and to take healthy ones

To ask for help

To recover from setbacks, self-esteem intact

To balance personal needs with those of a group

To recognize emotional reactions in others

To develop acceptable and effective ways of expressing feelings

To accept and appreciate differences in others

The value of helping others

The art of give-and-take

Self-advocacy

To cooperate with others

Patience

Responsibility for own life, e.g., making your own bed

How to leave this world a better place

KAMAJI

"**For two summers five of my friends and I,** all from the same Campfire Girls group, went to Camp Yalani in the San Bernardino Mountains. The second summer, one by one, each came down with pinkeye and was admitted to the infirmary. By the time I was the only healthy one left, I was pretty lonely. So I decided to rub dirt in my eye to make my eye pink. I was the sixth one to go to the infirmary, and they started calling me 'Pinky 6.' They put salve in our eyes and we couldn't open them for what seemed like all day. But we each had our own bed, and we were talking and laughing and just glad to be together again, pinkeye or no."

—Christine Trammell Balch, *Yalani*, 1963–64

Getting to Know Them

From a 1926 lecture by Elizabeth Kemper Adams, Educational Secretary of the Girl Scouts, in which she classified girls by type:

The imaginative girl, inclined to daydreaming. How may we harness her imagination to reality?

The know-it-all, bossy girl who wants to run things and be in the limelight and who often resents authority and control.

The shy, stay-by-herself girl who often thinks she is neglected and misunderstood.

The quarrelsome girl who has "tantrums" and flies off the handle.

The babyish girl, who wants to be petted and loved and who wants things done for her.

The girl who is always having "crushes."

The stolid, unresponsive girl, sometimes really dull, but not always.

The "bored" and oversophisticated girl, who thinks camp is "silly."

The restless, "bird-witted" girl, who tires quickly of things and leaves them half done.

The exceptionally bright girl, with not enough outlets for her abilities.

The so-called "average girl." How may we find her "bents" and bring them out?

SIGN NEAR FLAGPOLE AT MINNE WONKA

I COME HERE TO FIND MYSELF.
IT IS SO EASY TO GET LOST IN THE WORLD.

"I didn't feel I had to change, to be

WYONEGONIC

like other girls, in order to be appreciated."

—Julie Favreau Schwartz, *Little Notch*, 1966–73, 1979–89, 1995

"**When we were in our early teens,** we were very mean to a girl in our bunk who had very bad body odor. We all moved our cots to one side of the room and left her on the other side with the counselor."

—Janet Ehrlich Bettman, *Romaca*, early 1940s for 10 years

"How good you were at jacks was really important."
—Ellen Rubinoff DuPuy, *Winona*, 1956–65

HOW TO PLAY JACKS

RULES

You can use only one hand to toss the JACKS, pick up the JACKS, or pick up the BALL. Neither the BALL nor the JACKS may touch your other hand, body, or clothes while in play.

The BALL may bounce only once in a single play. If it bounces more than once, you lose your turn.

All JACKS must remain where they fall when scattered. You can only touch the JACKS you're trying to pick up.

Flip for Who Goes First. One by one, each player holds ten JACKS in her hand and tosses them a few inches into the air as she turns her hand over and tries to catch as many as she can. The player who drops the fewest JACKS goes first.

Let the Game Begin. Begin by throwing the JACKS out on the floor. Throw the ball into the air, pick up the correct number of JACKS, and, while letting the ball bounce just once, catch the ball while still holding the JACKS. Your turn continues until you miss the ball, miss the JACKS, move a JACK, or drop a JACK you've just picked up. Then you are out and it is the next person's turn. You work your way up from ONESIES to TENSIES.

On ONESIES, you pick up one JACK at a time until you've collected all ten. (You may put the JACKS you've collected in your other hand or on the ground before you try to collect more.) On TWOSIES, you pick them up two at a time. On THREE-SIES, you pick them up three at a time, with one left over. You pick up the leftover by itself. If you pick up the leftover before you've picked up all the evenly grouped JACKS, you are putting the horse before the cart and therefore must call "CART!" as you take the leftover JACK. On FOURSIES, there are, obviously, two groups of four and two JACKS in the "cart." FIVESIES has no cart. SIXSIES has one group of six and four in the cart. And so on.

If you throw the JACKS and two (or more) are touching, it is KISSIES, and you have the option of picking up the kissing JACKS and dropping them to spread them out.

BEYOND BASIC JACKS

Fancies are specialty rounds. At the start of a game, the players decide how many and what kinds of Fancies will be included.

Some Fancies are short: a simple chant with a certain pattern of activity that composes the whole Fancy. Some Fancies are long: a certain, trickier way of picking up the jacks that is performed from ONESIES to TENSIES.

A game might be "FLIP to TEN-SIES; three Fancies; one long, two short," meaning that players can FLIP as far as TENSIES but must play TEN-SIES back to ONESIES, then complete a long Fancy and two short Fancies in order to win.

SOME FANCIES

Eggs in the Basket You must pick up the jacks and move them to the other hand before grabbing the ball.

Crack the Eggs Scatter the jacks, toss the ball, pick up and CRACK (tap) the jacks on the floor. Catch the ball in the same hand.

Pigs in the Pen Instead of picking up the jacks, you push them into your opposite hand, which is cupped on the ground. You can lift the thumb and forefinger to let the pig(s) in, but the rest of your hand can't move.

Sheep over the Fence Rather than corral them, this time you jump them over the fence. Left hand and forearm are on the floor to create the fence. Scatter the jacks on one side of the fence, toss the ball, pick up one jack and place it over the fence. Catch the ball. The sheep cannot be thrown over the fence. Each must be placed on the playing surface.

ALOHA

"Even though my mother had told me
that girls mature at different rates, I felt upset because I was older than some of the girls in my bunk who already had bosoms and who had their period. I remember feeling that I wasn't competing well in this area."

—Ruth Gordon Hinerfeld, *Kear-Sarge, 1936–45*

THE OTHER SIDE

"A girl nicknamed Sid was the ringleader of our bunk. She was utterly manipulative and cruel, always thinking up strange tests for us to prove our loyalty.

Sid had a henchman and the two of them were forever plotting ways to embarrass girls they didn't like and planning horrible surprises for those who were different, i.e., fat, unattractive, or undistinguished horseback riders. This *Lord of the Flies* behavior made me understand that there are people who get pleasure from hurting others, and I learned to keep a low profile lest I become their next target."

—Eleanor Zimmer, *Wishe, 1965–66*

TAPAWINGO

" 'Cabin chat' happens right before bed every night.** The cabin group sits around a candle, and sometimes we begin by having each of us share the highlight of her day. Then one of the counselors asks a question that we each have to answer. The question might be 'What was the best day of your life so far?' or 'If you could have dinner with anyone, living or dead, who would it be?' or 'What's your greatest regret?' No one judges you, and no one will discuss your answer later with anyone. You can say whatever you feel, and dealing with those emotions in such a supportive place is exhilarating. There'll be chats where everyone is bawling their eyes out or where we're all laughing so hard we're about to burst and both are equally special."

— **Christine Provost,** *Chimney Corners, 1999–2001*

"Our director, Jocelyn, used to remind us that camp is full of choices, but doing nothing isn't one of them." —Mary Milne Marshall, *Glen Bernard, 1978–99*

ALOHA

BEDSIDE READING

PRE-1950

Anne of Green Gables, by Lucy M. Montgomery

Babbitt, by Sinclair Lewis

Movie magazines

Diary of a Young Girl, by Anne Frank

Goodbye, Mr. Chips, by James Hilton

Peter Rabbit, by Beatrix Potter

1950–80

The counselor's diary (and then felt guilty for years!)

Archie & Veronica comics

Trashy romance magazines

MAD magazine

Anything by Kahlil Gibran

Mademoiselle, the September college issue, which came out in early August

The Little Prince, by Antoine de Saint-Exupéry

A dog-eared, contraband copy of Grace Metalious's *Peyton Place,* read by flashlight

Never Love a Stranger, A Stone for Danny Fisher, The Carpetbaggers, Where Love Has Gone, all by Harold Robbins and all absolutely steamy

Everything You Always Wanted to Know About Sex—But Were Afraid to Ask, by David Reuben, M.D.

Valley of the Dolls, by Jacqueline Susann

Portnoy's Complaint, by Philip Roth

Catcher in the Rye, by J.D. Salinger

POST-1980

The counselor's diary (and then felt guilty for years!)

The Giving Tree, by Shel Silverstein

Archie comics

Everything Harry Potter

Seventeen

Teen People

YM

CosmoGIRL!

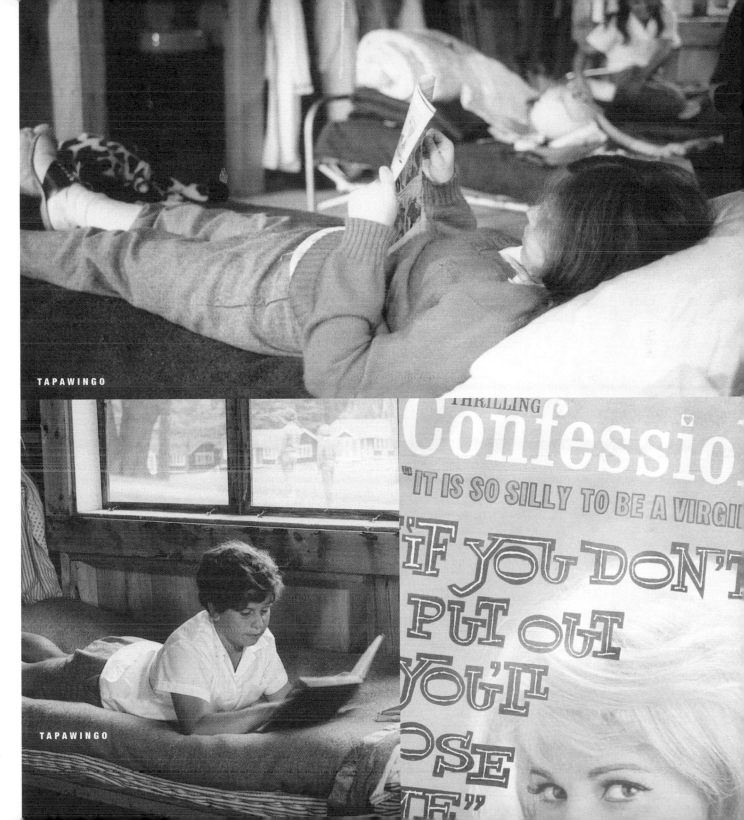

TAPAWINGO

TAPAWINGO

ONLY THE BEST NEED APPLY

In 1924, Camp Greystone proudly announced its "councillor list":

Twenty experienced councillors are carefully selected for their qualifications for leadership in the various activities of camp. Each councillor is a consecrated Christian young woman who possesses an attractive personality and loves young people. Each councillor is the companion of a group of four or five girls during the camping season, chaperoning groups of girls to and from camp, and is in charge of classes in her chosen activity at camp.

Head Councillor
Miss Janie McGaughey,
*Director of Young People's
Work, First Presbyterian
Church, Knoxville, Tennessee;
Agnes Scott College, Atlanta,
Georgia; The Biblical Seminary,
New York; Teacher of Bible,
Assembly Training School,
Richmond, Virginia*

Head Athletic Councillor
Miss Catherine Ruland
Wilson College

Swimming and Life Saving
Miss Mary Love McLure
Winthrop College

Swimming and Diving
Miss Nell Russell
Smith College

Land Sports
Miss Elizabeth Clanton
Wesleyan College

Canoeing and Boating
Miss Katherine Atwater
Smith College

Assistant Riding
Miss Frances Ohme
University of Alabama

Assistant Riding
Miss Clayre Ruland
Johns Hopkins

Aesthetic and Folk Dancing
Mrs. Theo. Price
Public Schools, Augusta, Georgia

Head of Music Department
Miss Margaret Funkhouser
Peabody Conservatory

Bible
Miss Grace Peake
Wilson College

Craft
Miss Dorothy Sevier
Drexel Institute

Basketry
Miss Katherine Wilson
Macon, Georgia

Rug Weaving
Miss Dorothy Franklin
Crossnore, North Carolina

Nature Study
Miss Margaret Whitten
Intermont College

Dietitian
Mrs. Lena Osborne
Dallas, Texas

Dramatics
Miss Ma'Nita Bullock
University of Georgia

Song Leader
Miss Katherine Foster
Washington University

Tutoring
Miss Elizabeth Askew
Agnes Scott College

Camp Mother
Mrs. Mamie McGaughey
Knoxville, Tennessee

Trained Nurse
Miss Allie Branson
Knoxville, Tennessee

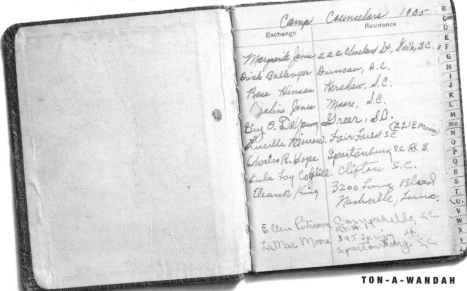

TON-A-WANDAH

WINONA

*Note from a Swatonah counselor to
the camp director, 1959*

1, 2, 3, 4, 5, 6, 7, 8, 9, 10, 11,
12 OOPS!

"Are you missing anyone?"
   was your cry;
Elbows perched in your classic
   "on porch pose."
Eyes gazing straight ahead
Waiting for *ME*!!!

What was I to do except to
   admit the truth.
Yes, Erica Groder was still at
   Fort Delaware and I was
   home at Swat with only 12
   of my charges.
How embarrassed I was, how
   foolish I felt . . . .

Your Special "GROUPIE"
Judi

57

KIPPEWA

"**Counselors were inviting us into a world adventure** they already enjoyed. They were prophets who called forth our best selves. They helped me up a mountain or a rock, taught me how to paddle or, my first year, how to put aside the broad-brimmed hat I wore, hoping that no one would notice me! They taught me how to smile at the world."

—Christine Amiot Carter, *Green Cove, 1969–79*

"**My counselor Gwen Park taught me** that life isn't always easy, so you have to figure out a way to make it work and to never give up. Fate was kind; our paths crossed again my rookie year of teaching in Port Arthur, Texas, and she became my mentor, sharing her teaching skills and secrets. We've kept in touch through phone calls and letters, and when my father died and I was truly devastated, she sent me red roses with a note: 'Don't focus on what you lost. Focus on what you *had.*' My life has been better due to her influence and guidance."

—Betty Harris Dunnam, *Kickapoo Kamp, 1952–55*

UNIDENTIFIED

"Counselors were role models for us. They were who we wanted to be when we grew up."

—Marilyn Pratt Rinehart, *Hickory Hill*, 1948–49

"My first summer as a bunk counselor, I'd been told to get to the train station early to greet my campers and their parents. One mother asked to speak to me privately. She said her daughter had not gotten her first period yet but probably would during camp, and would I please explain everything to her when the day came. This was my first job!"

—Ruth Jonas Gordon, *Crystal Lake, 1936–42*

BLUE RIDGE

KEEWANO

"A camper of mine felt so incredibly 'herself' and 'free' at camp that at night, after shower time, she would swing naked from the rafters, shouting: 'I AM SUPERWOMAN!'"

—Mary Moore Keever, *Illahee, 1987–2000*

WALDEN

ADVICE TO COUNSELORS

"Camp is for the campers."

"Try to develop an appreciation of the mystery, the marvel, the order and grandeur that can be felt in the out-of-doors. The purpose of camp life may be hard for the campers to understand or believe unless these qualities are demonstrated daily by the staff."

"Children sometimes find out at camp that it is easier and happier to learn than to pretend to know."

"Youth is a joyous time—not a sickness to be cured."

"A camper's behavior is always normal to her, although it may not be to the camp situation. There are causes behind every type of behavior. This doesn't mean that a counselor shouldn't seek to change it."

"Nagging and bribery only block the growth of campers."

"Salaries are not a matter for personal discussion, but strictly a matter of the counselor and the Directors. It is in bad taste, as well as in violation of your agreement, to discuss this matter with your friends or staff members."

Sing Along

Good morning to you.
Good morning to you.
You look kind of drowsy,
In fact you look lousy.
Is that any way
To start a new day?
Good morning to you.
Good morning to you.

"I didn't realize how much I owe to my camper years until I went back as a counselor. Adolescent girls are so fragile."

—Julia Altrocchi,
Wohelo, 1981–83, 1985, 1992–93

RED PINE

TAPAWINGO

A Place of Their Own

"Camp stories are the hardest to tell. All I know is that this place is pure delight—a miracle in the mountains. The days are the closest thing to heaven I can imagine. The children are healthy and happy, they laugh and actually roll down the hills for fun. They sing in the dining hall and climb up the apple trees to pick the apples and feed them to the horses and then to themselves. They have big eyes and little hands. They get in trouble for playing their little girl tricks. When I see them dancing, I am shown that a little girl is the most beautiful of all creations. They blush and learn to be ladies. They put their napkins in their laps and still catch frogs in the afternoon. Here they are alive and full of life.

They are special from the moment they arrive. The name tag their counselor gives them says, 'See, I already knew you were coming and I could hardly wait for you to arrive. We've carved out a place for you to be safe and free for five weeks of an otherwise hard year.' Here you go to sleep to the sound of the wind and a piano and wake to the smell of baking bread. It is safe—that is what I know of this place. Safe, even in the midst of the storms that seem to come like clockwork on the afternoons when camp needs the rain most.

The stories of camp cannot be told because they lie too deep. Years later a memory comes to a child and she remembers writing her name on a cabin wall: her claim that she was here, that her life matters and was transformed by a summer in the mountains. I love this place because it teaches that the spirit of a child is of infinite value. I love that people matter more than programs, that stillness is honored, that tradition is not forgotten, and that at least one part of the world slows down for a few weeks and basks in the light of each other and the God who made it all.

Every day, I am struck by the value of a life. At camp, more than anywhere else, I am struck by the seeming simplicity of any life of a child and the details of her day. The simplest action suddenly takes on great meaning. A name tag has eternal significance, a seat in the dining hall, her name in the *Green and Gold* book, a bunk that is hers, a trunk with her things carefully folded on opening day and filled with ceramics projects, notes, pictures, and memories on closing day. She leaves having spent time at the council fire ring, where for eighty years the trees have witnessed the presence of tiny lives waiting to see what happens next."

—Heather Brown Holleman,
Greystone, 1994–99

"**I grew up in the late 1940s and early '50s,** when roles for girls and women were really defined. But at camp I was exposed to free thought in terms of how our camp director, Rhoda, viewed herself as a woman and how she encouraged us. This was an area I had not been exposed to before: thinking of myself as someone with possibilities beyond how I looked or whom I could marry. *Who I was mattered.*

And then there was the way Rhoda carried herself; she seemed utterly comfortable with her body. In the late 1940s, when most women hid while they were pregnant, here was Rhoda pregnant and in a bathing suit, swimming with us in the lake. She was so natural, so different from my mother. This made a real impression on me."

—Ruthanne Carp Schlesinger, *Kear-Sarge, 1948–56*

"**There's a direct relationship** between the quality of the staff and the amount of stuff left in the lost-and-found at the end of the summer."

—Nancy Burns, *Waukeela, 1940–52*
(*staff 1976–80, director 1981–90, staff 2001–02*)

"Camp was wonderful, with real college women as counselors and a terrific staff that could teach you anything you wanted to learn."

— Judy Page Horton, *Arrowhead*, 1954–55

FOREST ACRES

Chapter 3

SO MUCH TO DO, SO LITTLE TIME

For a tomboy like me, camp was exciting because I was around other athletes. But on the softball field, I got as much pleasure from my teammates who were just learning to catch (and hold on to) a pop fly. They believed I could pitch like the wind, so I often did.

Sure, no one wanted to be the last girl picked for a team, but winning was never the really important part. We'd battle on the volleyball court and then walk away arm in arm. Camp was a series of moments that taught me that I don't lose anything if *she* succeeds; another's

WYONEGONIC

success doesn't diminish me. At home, in school, competition was more directly related to achievement: getting *the* best grades, *the* most honors, *the* most popular boy. At camp I learned the truth: I am my own competition.

Girls wanted to improve their skills, but they were encouraged to do so without reference to the abilities of those around them. And there were so many things to excel at: good sportsmanship and earnest cheerleading, drama and arts and crafts. But the real secret was that it was okay to be average at everything. It didn't matter.

Putting on a dance recital or a play was as much a team effort as any sporting event. My last year as a camper, I was cast as the manager in *Damn Yankees,* which meant I had to sing "You've Gotta Have Heart." I protested. I was uncharacteristically cranky. I was sure I'd fall flat; certainly my voice would. But my bunkmates Lois DeVita and Tobe Taylor would be up there with me, and soon the silliness of learning overly ambitious choreography while figuring out how to modulate our froggy tones began to be fun. We brought the house down that Saturday night, not because of the notes we hit or missed but because we were the most senior campers and we were being silly and playful and brave. In my whole life I'd never sung a solo until that show. I've never sung one again. But that night, on that stage, I was a star.

"I was more uninhibited than I'd ever been anywhere in my life."
—Susan Moldof Goldman Rubin, *Kear-Sarge, 1948–53*

ROBINDEL

7:15   REVEILLE

7:45   FLAG RAISING

8:00   BREAKFAST & MORN-
ING ANNOUNCEMENTS

8:45   CLEANUP (FOLLOWED
BY BUNK INSPECTION)

9:30   FIRST PERIOD

10:30   SECOND PERIOD

11:45   GENERAL SWIM

12:45   LUNCH & MAIL

1:30   REST HOUR

2:30   THIRD PERIOD

3:30   MILK & COOKIES

3:45   FOURTH PERIOD

5:00   GENERAL SWIM

6:00   FLAG LOWERING

6:15   DINNER & MAIL

7:00   CANTEEN

7:30   EVENING ACTIVITY

9:00   LIGHTS OUT—JUNIORS

9:45   LIGHTS OUT—SENIORS

"While I wasn't the team leader, at least I could be on the team."

—Judi Kahn Zukor, *Kear-Sarge,* 1959–66

TAPAWINGO

WALDEN

GREYSTONE

WAUKEELA

The Hero of My Youth

"**On the first night of camp, each new girl was called forward to draw a piece of colored** paper out of a hat, to determine which tribe she'd belong to for all her camping days. As my cabin-mates were called up, I could hear the older girls in the audience: 'Ooh, she's so cute!' or 'She's just darling!' And then there was me. At nine, I was a gangly kid, all legs and feet, nothing particularly cute about me, and I predicted, correctly, that my appearance would evoke no such response.

My next summer, Karen Schrunk, who was about sixteen and one of the tribal leaders, noticed me. She was the hero of my youth; our initial encounter, a turning point in my life. Karen, an accomplished athlete, asked if she could show me a few things, like how to throw and catch the kickball. After she'd worked with me, she suggested I try out for the upcoming kickball game and I made the team. Even though I was no star player, what mattered was that Karen had seen me as someone having potential. She gave me skills and confidence that I would never have otherwise possessed. Every summer thereafter I tried out for every game—even though I didn't 'find' my coordination until I was thirteen or fourteen.

There was something else that summer that changed me. At the end of the six-week session, a secret-ballot vote of the entire camp elected one camper from each age group to receive an Honor Camper award. That summer I was the Junior Honor Camper. I don't know if people voted for me because Karen had anointed me, but I remember feeling I'd have to do my best to stand up to the scrutiny of the entire camp. It was something I took very seriously."

—Jane Ragsdale,
*Mystic, 1966–69 (June terms);
Fern, 1970; Heart O' the Hills, 1969–72,
1974 (July terms) (director, 1977–present)*

TAPAWINGO

"I NEVER DID **THAT** BEFORE . . ."

Skinny-dipping before breakfast (and hiding the clothes of the girls who did)

Annual initiation of new campers (often on July 4, after which everyone was considered an old camper)

Listening to announcements at mealtime

Ghost stories

Bull sessions

Calling the bathroom the john, greenies, teba, or biffy

Signing your name in shoe polish on the interior bunk walls

Putting on a damp bathing suit

Almost freezing to death the day of the senior lifesaving exam

Biting into a huge fireball

Singing "99 Bottles of Beer on the Wall" on every bus trip

Whispering after lights out

Being homesick

Playing in the rain without a coat, hat, or rubbers

Making friends out of strangers

Not feeling silly for crying

Singing during meals

Bathing in the lake

Not caring about bad hair days

Writing jingles about each counselor

Signing pillowcases at the end of the summer

Going to reunions

"I went from being a wimp to a winner."

—Betty Harris Dunnam, *Kickapoo Kamp*, 1952–55

GREYSTONE

Prayer of a Sportsman

Dear Lord, in the battle that
    goes on through life,
I ask but a field that is fair,
A chance that is equal with all
    in the strife,
A courage to strive and to dare;
And if I should win, let it be by
    the code
With my faith and my honor
    held high.
And if I should lose, let me
    stand by the road
And cheer as the winners go by.

And Lord, may my shouts be
    ungrudging and clear,
A tribute that comes from the
    heart,
And let me not cherish a snarl
    or a sneer
Or play any sniveling part.
Let me say, "There they ride, on
    whom laurels bestowed,

Since they played the game
    better than I."
Let me stand with a smile by
    the side of the road
And cheer as the winners go by.

So grant me to conquer,
    if conquer I can,
By proving my
    worth in the
    fray,
But teach me to
    lose like a regular
    man
And not like a craven, I pray.
Let me take my hat off to the
    warriors who strode
To victory splendid and high,
Yet teach me to stand by the
    side of the road
And cheer as the winners go by.

—Berton Braley

ALOHA

KEYSTONE

GIRLS VACATION FUND CAMP

"**I had polio when I was nine,** so I had to learn to walk a second time. My running was measured and could only be sustained for short sprints. Years later I was part of a relay race at Brookwood, and was so caught up in the excitement of winning and the joy of running that I just let myself go."

—H. Lisa Kimmel Steele Roach,
Brookwood, 1953–59

KINIYA

MATAPONI

GIRLS VACATION FUND MISSION STATEMENT

To empower girls to become strong, productive, and caring contributors to their communities through outdoor experiential education, year round mentoring, and leadership training

BASKETBALL

CAMP TON-A-WANDAH CREED

I BELIEVE IN LIFE AS A GREAT GAME.

I BELIEVE I MUST UPHOLD THE COLORS IN GOOD FAITH; NEVER ALIBI, BUT PLAY THE GAME FAIR AND SQUARE TO WIN.

I BELIEVE IN FRIENDSHIPS AND THE JOY OF SERVICE FOR OTHERS.

I BELIEVE IN THE FLOWERS, THE SUNSHINE AND THE CLOUDS, THE GLORY OF THE SUNSET, AND IN EVERY BEAUTIFUL THING.

I BELIEVE IN THE WHISPER OF LEAVES, THE STRENGTH OF GREAT TREES, THE CALL OF BIRDS, THE INSPIRATION OF TOWERING MOUNTAINS AND IN EVERY GREAT LESSON NATURE TEACHES.

I BELIEVE IN MOMENTS OF SILENCE, AND NIGHTS OF QUIET WHEN A GIRL CAN QUESTION HER SOUL AND FIND HERSELF.

I BELIEVE IN LOVE AND I BELIEVE IN FAITH TO THE HIGHEST.

I BELIEVE IN THE GUIDING SPIRIT OF YOUTH THAT LOOKS UPWARD AND FINDS THE BEST IN LIFE.

I BELIEVE IN MY BETTER SELF BECAUSE I BELIEVE IN GOD.

ALOHA

KAMAJI

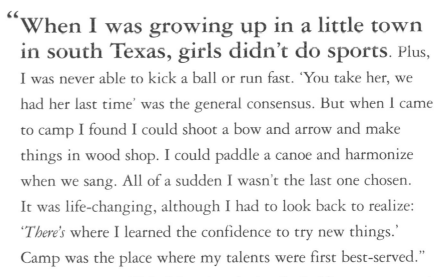

"**When I was growing up in a little town in south Texas, girls didn't do sports.** Plus, I was never able to kick a ball or run fast. 'You take her, we had her last time' was the general consensus. But when I came to camp I found I could shoot a bow and arrow and make things in wood shop. I could paddle a canoe and harmonize when we sang. All of a sudden I wasn't the last one chosen. It was life-changing, although I had to look back to realize: '*There's* where I learned the confidence to try new things.' Camp was the place where my talents were first best-served."

—Nicia Oakes, *Arrowhead, 1961–65 (director, 1975–2001); presently director of Honey Creek*

The Warmth of Icy Waters

"I spent my childhood summers immersed in icy waters. I was a reluctant swimmer; given half a chance, I would have stayed behind in my cabin, warm and dry, playing jacks or curled up cozily in my jelly roll, reading a story about girl detectives.

But ours was a no-nonsense camp, proud of building character in the little city girls who were shipped to it by overnight train from Grand Central Station. Vega, the camp was called, and they told us proudly it was named after the brightest star in the summer night sky. Vega sat on Echo Lake, seventeen miles southwest of Augusta, Maine, as the loon flies. At Vega, shirkers were not allowed. So, like it or not, we were in those loon lakes rain or shine, rotating lap after lap of sidestroke, breaststroke, and crawl. The respite of elementary backstroke was our officially sanctioned chance to rest.

The summer we turned eleven, seven of us were allowed to swim the two miles from junior camp to senior camp. This was the crowning point of the season. As juniors, we looked forward to the status of being one of the girls actually living in the exalted world of Senior; reaching Senior was as far as our maps of the future went.

We jumped off the wooden dock and swam far out into the heart of the lake, accompanied by two serious counselors in a rowboat. There was no hint of competition in the swim. Each girl swam alone, but it was the joint effort of old pals and it linked us forever. Tess and Laura and Peggy and Leslie and Jane and Lory and me. We had practiced for weeks, doing lap after lap between the old mildewed wooden docks of junior camp. Now we were set free. Opening my eyes in the middle of the lake, I saw that the water held no hint of blue or even green. I could do no more than conjecture at the distance to the marshy lake bottom, which I knew must somewhere exist. But for me, the black water was as deep as the sky was high and no more had a finite bottom than did the sky have a cover on it.

We swimmers had no thought of failure. We were sure of ourselves and of one another. How long did the swim last? An hour? Two? We all made it.

Arriving at the dock of senior camp, we climbed up the wobbly metal ladder one after the other, as proud as if we had swum the Channel. We undid the chin straps and pulled off our latex caps. All the way on the swim we had been agile; now, sitting in a semicircle with our knees crossed, wrapped in towels, our legs turned to jelly and our arms felt heavy as stones. Years later, when we became senior campers for real, we knew we had never been more senior than we were on that dock, bonded and happy.

These days I swim in pools. But half a lifetime away, I can still turn my face to the sky and gaze at the white clouds of memory playing hide-and-seek with the pine trees. I wish I could turn my head just once and find Leslie or Peggy, Jane or Lory, Tess or Laura beside me, coming up for breath. I have a photo of us chubby swimmers, pasted crookedly into my camp scrapbook. Each has an arm around her buddy and the other raised in triumph."

—Helen Schary Motro,
Vega, 1957–63

"I'm not sure how much I loved being at a girls' camp. My swimming seemed to be mostly about taking the route to the boys' camp."

—H. Lisa Kimmel Steele Roach, *Brookwood*, 1953–59

WOHELO

"At camp I had more of a sense of belonging than anywhere else in the world." —Eleanor Westbrook Beckman, *Illahee*, 1952–59

CLEARWATER

TON-A-WANDAH

ARCADIA

KEAR-SARGE

NICOLET

"I was always worried about swimming, because as a little kid I'd had ear surgery and been told not to put my head underwater. But when we were older, one of our activities was to swim the mile across the lake, and one summer I was determined to try. Everyone set out; I did, too. Dusk came and everyone else had finished and was headed for dinner, I was still swimming that lake. Face it, I should have been hauled out of that water, but I'll never forget the feeling of triumph when I finally made it and it didn't matter how long it took. The counselors rowing alongside me missed most of dinner, but they stayed with me. And when I got to the dining hall nobody put me down; they actually stood and sang to me."

—Susan Moldof Goldman Rubin,
Kear-Sarge, 1948–53

CAMP KEA
AN
THE SUNAPEE WA
THIS IS TO CI
MARA C
HAS SUCCESSFU
Exper
HAVING PASSED TH
CAMP KE
DATE 8-22-6

The person whose name appears on this certificate has completed a swimmer course and has passed the following tests:

1. 100 yds. breast stroke
2. 100 yds. side stroke
3. 100 yds. back crawl, crawl or trudgen crawl
4. 50 yds. back swim (legs alone)
5. Turns (for closed course)
6. Surface dive
7. Tread water (1 minute)
8. Plunge dive
9. Running front dive
10. 10-minute swim

B.A. Rheobald
Instructor's Signature

Concord N.H.
Name of Chapter

Le Roy E. Wood
Chapter Representative

23   Cert. 1388 (Rev. 3-52)

CAMP SAYINGS

Everyone needs a buddy. BUDDIES!!!!!!!!!!!!!!

You have to learn to take it.

Do over!

Cooties!

One-two-three SHHHHH-HHHHHHHH!

Side out and rotate!

Does your chewing gum lose its flavor on your bed-post overnight?

Two-four-six-eight/ Who do we appreciate?/ *(name of person said twice)/* YEAH!

I double-dog dare ya!

What makes *you* such a P.C. (privileged camper)?

Counselor's pet!

When the hand goes up, the mouth goes closed.

Take turns.

Leave only footprints; take only pictures.

Spiders are good—they eat all the other bugs.

Nature has feelings, too.

It's okay to be homesick

It only takes a spark to get a fire going.

The best of each for the good of all.

Last one in is a rotten egg!

A SHORT COURSE IN LIFESAVING

From Campfire Girls Book of Aquatics (1925)

Head Carry. Cover subject's ears with palms of your hands, so that your middle finger rests along her jaw-bone on each side. Holding her chin high to arch subject's back, swim, using frog kick or vertical or reverse scissors kick.

In the latter, the hips are tipped slightly to one side and legs separated as in side stroke, but with upper leg opening backward and under leg forward, reversing the ordinary scissors kick to avoid fouling the subject.

Cross-Chest Carry. From position back of subject, reach across her shoulder and chest, placing your hand under her farther arm-pit. (Shoulder blade is more comfortable if you can reach it.) Hold subject so that your hip is directly under center of her back, and her shoulder tight under your arm-pit. Swim on your side, using scissors kick and

side-arm pull. Keep her head out of the water and hold her firmly in place with elbow against her shoulder. This

carry is a favorite among lifesavers because subject is completely under control.

Hair Carry. From position back of subject, place your hand at crown of her head, your fingers toward her forehead, grasping a handful of hair. With your hand in this position she will not roll over. Swim on your side with side-arm pull and scissors kick. Keep your holding arm straight. This

carry is especially easy to learn and is optional with the Arm-Lock Carry.

Tired Swimmer's Carry. In approaching, simply swim to the subject, telling her to lie on her back and place her hands on your shoulders, with her arms straight and feet spread apart. Swim breast stroke, using either frog or scissors kick.

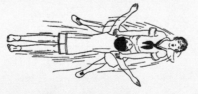

Watch subject's face. This carry is intended only for assisting a person who has become tired. It should never be used on a struggling person.

KAMAJI

"Camp was the place where my talents were first best-served." —Nicia Oakes, *Arrowhead* 1961–65

KINIYA

FERNWOOD

ALOHA

"I was a swimmer, but at home that didn't mean anything to anyone. At camp, people recognized and appreciated me as a really fine racer. So at the socials, if I didn't dance with many boys (or even if I did), it didn't matter. It was my split times, not my dance card, that people thought of when they thought of me."

—Nancy Feingold Palmer, *Kear-Sarge, 1958–65*

"At camp it didn't matter a whole lot if you came in last."
—Katherine Bisbee Eldridge, *Natarswi*, 1965–71

WE-HA-KEE

MUDJEKEEWIS

WOHELO

"At twelve or thirteen, I was finally learning how to sail. We were taught the terminology and fundamentals in the boathouse before we were allowed on the boat. I knew I didn't understand all the nomenclature, but I figured I could handle a boat, so out I went. Luckily the wind was mild and I wasn't moving very much. I heard the instructor yelling at me to 'FALL OFF,' to get out of irons, so naturally I jumped off the boat. Later, when she asked me why I'd done that, I explained: 'You *told* me to fall off.' Eventually I turned into a fairly competent sailor, although I understand this incident is still a favorite camp story thirty-five years later."

—Susan Glazer-Belgrad, *Nicolet, 1964–70*

RED PINE CAMP MOTTO

To HELP EACH GIRL DEVELOP HER FULL POTENTIAL WHILE ACCEPTING HER LIMITATIONS.

ALOHA

RUNOIA

"Our canoeing director, Hartzell Lyon, was a tough fellow who wore safari fatigues and whose approval meant a great deal. On my first attempt at paddling a straight mile, I arrived back at the dock to his smile. I knew I'd really done something."

—Caroline McNair, *Minne Wonka, 1959–68*

UNIDENTIFIED

TON-A-WANDAH

THE TIPPY TEST

Do you remember your first tippy test? Usually that's a story in itself.

The purpose of the tippy test is to really "get it" that the canoe will float and NOT SINK when it's full of water. You need to know at the bone level that if your canoe gets full of water and even if you've lost your paddles, you can stay in it and paddle by hand. You might not choose to, but you can. This experience builds a feeling of safety in learning to paddle as a beginner.

You paddle out a hundred feet or more from shore, stow your paddles under the crossbars, or thwarts, so they're less apt to swim away, and TIP THE CANOE OVER so it fills up with water. THIS ISN'T EASY, in case you thought it was, especially with some makes of canoe. We usually had to stand on one gunwale (edge) of the canoe and pull on the opposite gunwale in order to pull the thing over. This built our confidence. At this point almost everyone gets laughing hysterically, especially while trying to get the hang of sort of lizarding back into the canoe. She's floating, all right, but when pushed in any direction she behaves abominably, wallowing down, rolling over again after you've just gotten her right side up, and generally defying you in an infuriating, passive manner. Finally you and the canoe get it together. You are sitting gingerly in the bottom, up to your waist in water and paddling fiercely with both hands. The canoe is proceeding at a moderate and dignified pace, her own speed, pretty much regardless of your energy output. So relax! You've won and passed your tippy test, at least as soon as you get back to shore and dump her out.

—Jane Ingraham Thomas,
Camp Natarswi History (1994)

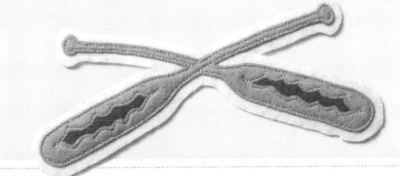

HOW TO MAKE A TREASURE BOX

What you'll need:

50–60 Popsicle sticks
Wood glue

1. To make the base of the treasure box, line up enough Popsicle sticks so that you can glue a stick across each end of the lined-up sticks (A).

2. Make a square out of four Popsicle sticks (B).

3. Make about six more of the squares you made in step 2, then glue them together to make the sides of your box.

4. Glue together the two pieces you have made so far (the base and the sides).

A

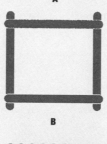

B

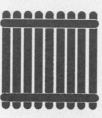

C

5. Make a lid for the box by repeating step 1, but glue the two end sticks into place closer to the center so they will fit inside the two horizontal sticks on top of your box (C). This will allow your lid to fit snugly on the box.

6. Paint your treasure box and/or decorate it by gluing a combination of feathers, shells, and things found in the garden to the top of it.

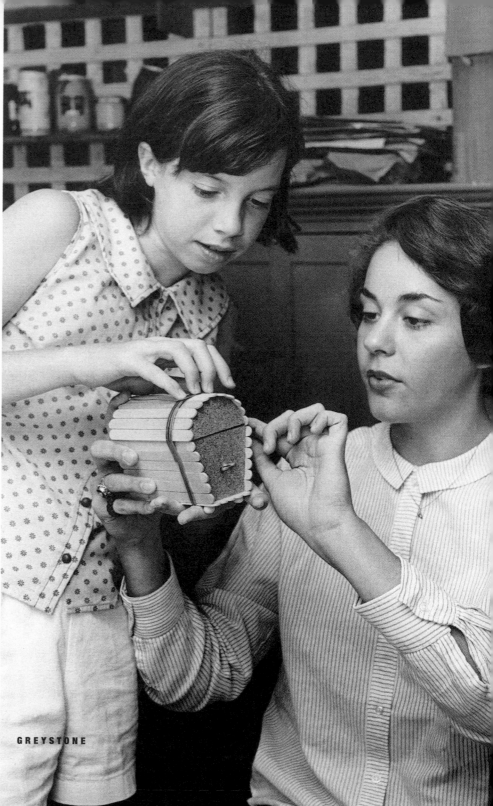

GREYSTONE

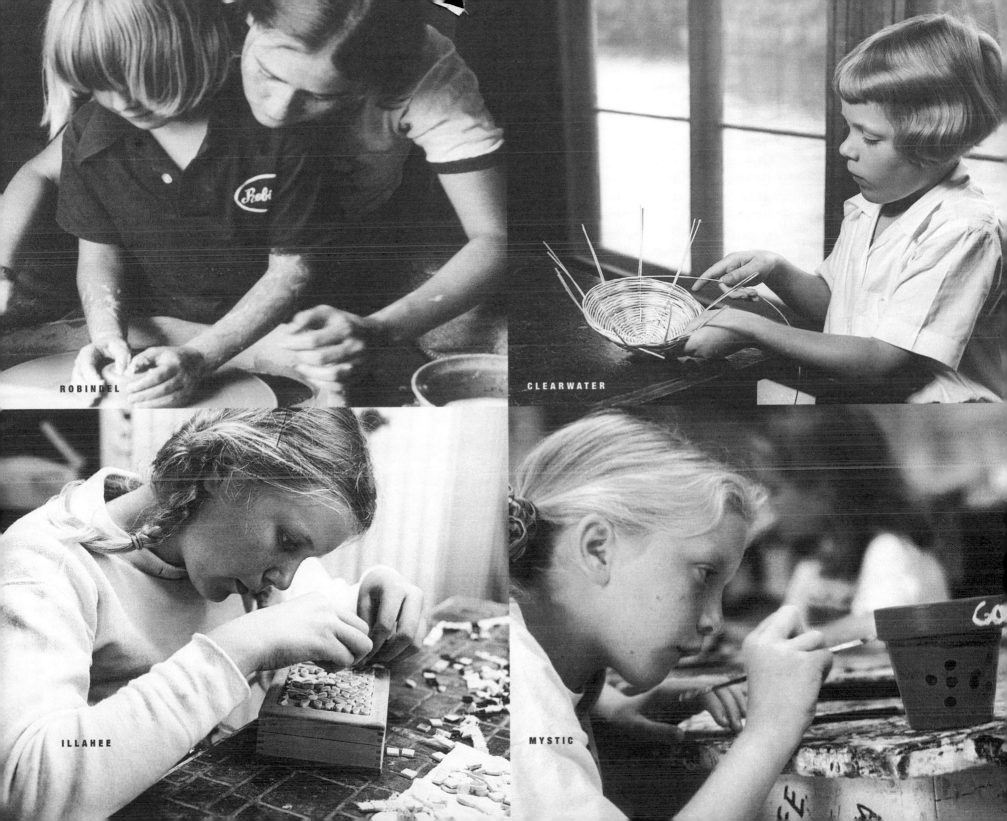

ROBINDEL

CLEARWATER

ILLAHEE

MYSTIC

> "I made so many diamond-stitched lanyards. Where are they now?"
> —Patricia Bileti Mussio, *Clear Lake, 1946–48*

ILLAHEE

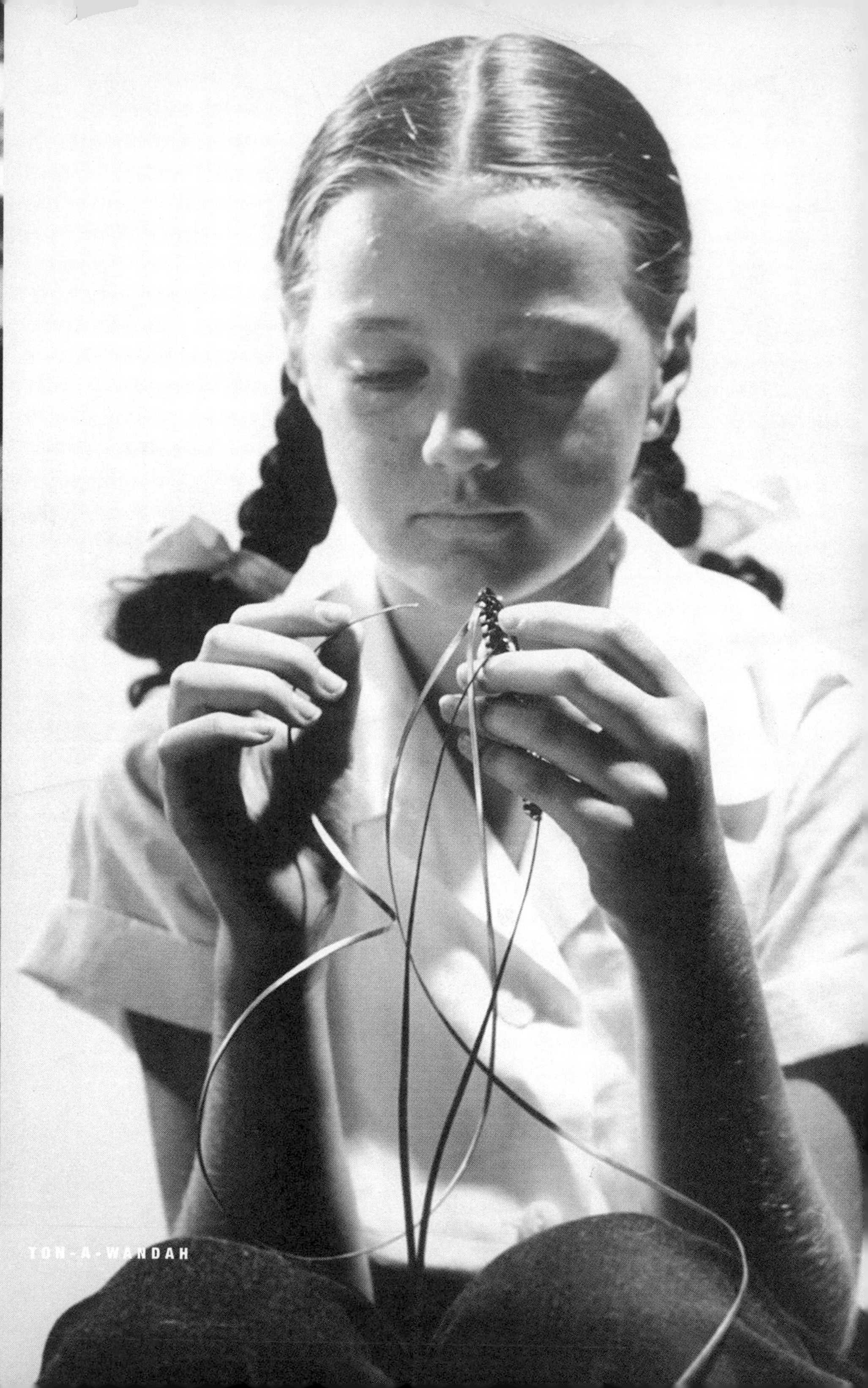

TON-A-WANDAH

HOW TO MAKE A LANYARD

From a brochure of the Pyrotex Corp., Leominster, Massachusetts (1955)

To start your lanyard, cut 3 yards of two contrasting colors of gymp. Draw the two strands through the eye of the swivel snap. It may be necessary to open the eye slightly and to bevel the ends of the lace to get it through.

1. Hang or tie the swivel snap on a nail or any firm object at a convenient working height (Fig. 1). Adjust lace so snap is in exact center and all four ends are together.

2. Arrange the strands as shown in Fig. 2, and count from left to right numbering them from 1 to 4.

3. Hold the center strands, 2 and 3, with the forefinger and thumb of the right hand. Take strand 4 with the left hand (Fig. 3) and bring around the back to the left and forward to the front between strands 1 and 2 (Fig. 4). Fold over strand 2 so that it lies parallel to strand 3 (Fig. 5). Draw all strands tight.

4. Hold the center strands, 2 and 4, with the forefinger and thumb of the left hand. Take strand 1 with the right hand (Fig. 6) and bring around the back to the right and forward to the front between strands 3 and 4 (Fig. 7). Fold over strand 4 so that

it lies parallel to strand 2 (Fig. 8). Draw all strands tight.

5. Continue braiding, repeating steps 3 and 4 alternately (Figs. 3 to 8). Remember that the working strand (the one that is woven into the others) is always the uppermost outside strand either on the right or the left.

6. Continue the round braid until the strands are 9 inches long. End with an overhand knot. Hold the lanyard in the left hand and tie the two left strands over the two right strands (Fig. 9). Be sure that strands are flat and neat before tightening the knot (Fig. 10).

7. At this point you switch to the square braid. Hold the lanyard in the left hand, upside down so that the strands fall apart, and renumber them from 1 to 4 (Fig. 10).

8. Fold strand 1 over strand 2, leaving a small loop (Fig. 11). Hold in position with the forefinger of the left hand. Hold each succeeding strand in position in the same way after each step.

9. Fold strand 2 over strand 1 (Fig. 12).

(continued on next page)

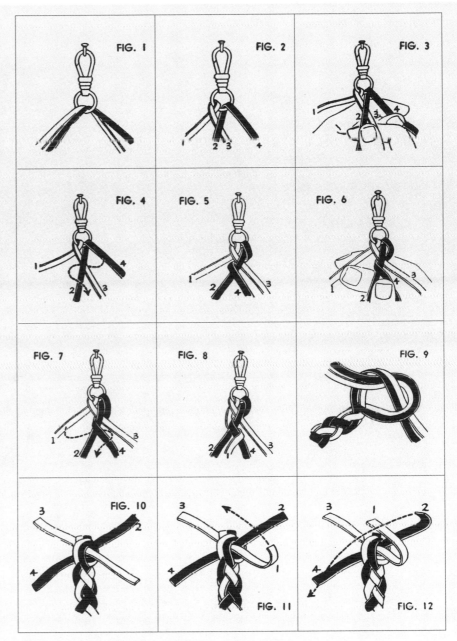

10. Fold strand 3 over strand 2 (Fig. 13).

11. Fold strand 4 over strand 3 and through the loop formed at the beginning (Fig. 14). Leave the stitch slightly loose (Fig. 15).

12. Form the loop of the lanyard by passing swivel snap through the center of the square braid just formed (Fig. 16). Tighten the braid slightly.

13. Slide the square braid along the lanyard every few stitches to be certain it is not too tight. Keep it uniform and neat.

14. Continue the square braid, using the lanyard as a core, until the strands are 4 inches long. Renumber the strands after each stitch and then follow steps 9 to 12 (Figs. 11 to 15).

15. At this point you switch to the Terminal Turk's Head. In order to form a Terminal Turk's Head, leave the last stitch of the square braid slightly loose. Renumber the strands from 1 to 4 as shown in Fig. 16.

16. Hold the braid in the left hand. Bring strand 1 under strand 2 and up through the center (Fig. 17). Leave this strand slightly loose. All strands of the Terminal Turk's Head are to be tightened when the ending is complete.

17. Bring strand 2 under strand 3 and up through the center (Fig. 18).

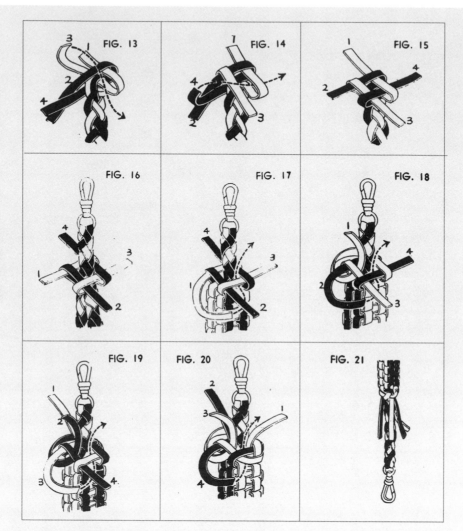

FIG. 13 FIG. 14 FIG. 15 FIG. 16 FIG. 17 FIG. 18 FIG. 19 FIG. 20 FIG. 21

18. Bring strand 3 under strand 4 and up through the center (Fig. 19).

19. Bring strand 4 under strands 1 and 2 and up through the center (Fig. 20).

20. Tighten the strands one at a time, starting with strand 1. Tighten sufficiently to form a neat Terminal Turk's Head but loose enough to slide easily over the lanyard. Be certain that none of the strands are twisted. Then clip off the ends of the strands, leaving a tassel of about 1 inch (Fig. 21). This completes the lanyard.

> **"When I was eleven, I didn't attend Campfire Girl camp** because I had no one to go with. After that, I resolved to never again lose out on an experience just because I had no one to go with me."
>
> —Barbara Jean Rioux Novak, *Sherwood, 1942–48*

WYONEGONIC

> "At home and in school there was pressure to get stellar grades, to act a certain way, to look a certain way, to dress a certain way. The pressure came from my parents, my teachers, my peers, and even from me.
>
> But then I would get to camp, where girls would be wearing Birkenstocks and T-shirts. They would get up in the morning and go to breakfast without brushing their hair. I went for days without looking in the mirror. I was happy, which was pretty amazing for a teenager."
>
> —Kendall Waite, *Red Pine*, 1986–96, 1999–2001

NORTHWAY LODGE

ARCADIA

"My mother had told me that if a ball is thrown, I should get out of the way because, God forbid, it could hit me in the face. And then what? So at camp I spent my time in the theater. Was I doing anything really big? No. But whatever it was, it was enough for me to grab onto."

—Nancy Edman Feldman, *Kear-Sarge, 1949–51*

THE PLEDGE OF A KICKAPOO KAMPER

KIND TO OTHERS

INTENT UPON DUTY

COURTEOUS TO ALL

KINDRED IN SPIRIT

ALWAYS READY

PUNCTUAL EVER

OBEDIENT ALWAYS

OBLIVIOUS OF SELF

ILLAHEE

MATAPONI

ILLAHEE

ALOHA

Illahee, 1931

Dear Mother,
The other night the BLUES gave a party. After the party we went to the lodge and danced. I danced awhile and then had to hold Gigi's hand. She got a bee sting and her hand was swollen way up. She couldn't move it so I had to hold it. Before we went to the lodge we had a play. There was the lover and girl as usual. There was a father, too. He came in and shot the lover and then the girl shot her father and herself. All during the play the only word they spoke was "Oh!" It was awful funny. I wore my sailor suit. I have not worn my dress since I have been up here. At the party Gigi wore Sara's white ducks.

Love,
Betsy

"**At age ten I had the distinction** of being one of two juniors to appear in the Senior Big Show, *The Music Man,* as Winthrop, the little lisping boy who sings 'Gary, Indiana.' This made me a bit of a camp celebrity." —Andrea Brown, *Mataponi, 1960–68*

BERNADETTE

LAUGH QUIET SYMPATH CLAP

"The summer of 1961, when I was fourteen, our group was to try out for song leader of the 'BIG' teams. Even though I felt I could do a great job, I was too shy to try out. But all of us agreed to watch the goings-on.

At the very last minute, my best friend decided to try out. I knew I was more musical than she was and that at least I had a sense of rhythm. Her audition was not very good. Afterwards they asked if anyone else wanted to try. I don't know what came over me, but my hand went up, and next thing I knew, I was leading everyone in song. To this day I'm amazed because I know how nervous and scared I was and how much courage it took.

Two days later, they announced the teams and I was chosen. As a result, I really came out of my shell and was elected captain my final year. It was an amazing transformation. I know that gathering up the courage to try out that day was a defining moment that impacted the rest of my life." —Jill Grayson Finkelstein, *Tripp Lake, 1957–63, 1965*

KICKAPOO KAMP

TAPAWINGO

"I learned that my voice, indistinguishable from Diana Ross's to my ears, did not sound like Diana Ross's to anyone else."

—Alice Jeanne Glick Meshbane, *O-Tahn-Agon, 1965–68, 1971–72*

TON-A-WANDAH

CAMP
ILLAHEE
1940

SIXTH
PLACE

ILLAHEE

WALDEN

ROCKY MOUNTAIN RANCH

"After five years of getting a nervous stomach** every Monday, Wednesday, and Friday before horseback riding, I realized I didn't have to ride and that it was okay if I didn't. What a liberating experience that was!"

—Holly Louise Carlisle, *Kineowatha*, 1966, 1968–74

"One hot, humid day we were mucking stalls** and moving the manure pile (which was about ten feet wide and ten feet high) by truck to another camp location. I don't remember how it got started, but we had a great manure fight with horse apples flying through the air, falling down shirts, and being rubbed into hair. When we finally finished moving the pile, we walked down to the swim docks, all brown and stinky, and jumped in the lake."

—Wendy E. Jones, *Northern Hills & Black Hawk*, 1976–81

WALDEMAR

ALOHA

"**My greatest accomplishment at camp** was being recognized for successfully identifying poisonous mushrooms and grasses on our nature walks. My chamois scarf was stamped with a picture of a mushroom and grasses, and I said, 'Nisha shin,' which meant 'Thank you' in some native tongue."

—Carol Keyser Mercer,
Songadeewin Wigwam of the Keewaydin Camps, 1938–41

"**I sent rolls of film home,** and when my mom saw the pictures of me holding a snake, she called the camp to check on me. It was a simple garden snake, but in her mind city kids were not supposed to hold snakes."

—Gina Magrino, *Brady Kaufman 1974–77*

ARCADIA

WYONEGONIC

"Camp provided the security of knowing that I could venture farther than my hometown and find new friends and experiences."

—Deborah Parker Gibbs, *Green Cove, 1968–79*

WYONEGONIC

Sing Along

(*Tune: "Ain't Gonna Rain No More"*)

The peppiest camp I ever saw,
It never came a-pokin'.
If I could tell you the pep it had,
You'd think I was a-jokin'.

It's not the pep in the pepper
  pot
Or the pep in the popcorn
  popper;
It's not the pep in the mustard
  jar
Or the pep in the vinegar
  stopper.

It's good old-fashioned P-E-P,
The pep you cannot doubt.
(*Camp name! Camp name!*)
The peppiest camp around!

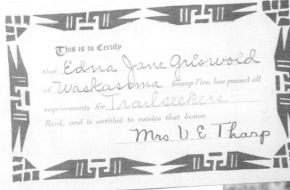

This is to Certify that *Edna Jane Griswold* of *Waskasina* Camp Fire, has passed all requirements for *Trailseekers* Rank, and is entitled to receive that honor.

Mrs. V. E. Tharp

KINIYA

KICKAPOO KAMP

IF YOU'RE HAPPY AND YOU KNOW IT

If you're happy and you know it,
    clap your hands (CLAP! CLAP!)
If you're happy and you know it,
    then your life will surely show it
If you're happy and you know it,
    clap your hands (CLAP! CLAP!)

If you're happy and you know it,
    stamp your feet (STAMP! STAMP!)
If you're happy and you know it,
    stamp your feet (STAMP! STAMP!)
If you're happy and you know it,
    then your life will surely show it
If you're happy and you know it,
    stamp your feet (STAMP! STAMP!)
Clap your hands (CLAP! CLAP!)

If you're happy and you know it,
    wear a smile (SMILE!)
If you're happy and you know it,
    wear a smile (SMILE!)
If you're happy and you know it,
    then your life will surely show it.
If you're happy and you know it,
    wear a smile (SMILE!)
Stamp your feet (STAMP! STAMP!)
Clap your hands (CLAP! CLAP!)

If you're happy and you know it,
    say amen (AMEN!)
If you're happy and you know it,
    say amen (AMEN!)

If you're happy and you know it,
    then your life will surely show it.
If you're happy and you know it,
    say amen (AMEN!)
Wear a smile (SMILE!)
Stamp your feet (STAMP! STAMP!)
Clap your hands (CLAP! CLAP!)

If you're happy and you know it,
    sing a song (TRA LA LA!)
If you're happy and you know it,
    sing a song (TRA LA LA!)
If you're happy and you know it,
    then your life will surely show it.
If you're happy and you know it,
    sing a song (TRA LA LA!)
Say amen (AMEN!)
Wear a smile (SMILE!)
Stamp your feet (STAMP! STAMP!)
Clap your hands! (CLAP! CLAP!)

JOHN JACOB JINGELHEIMER SCHMIDT

John Jacob Jingelheimer Schmidt,
His name is my name, too.
And whenever we go out
The people always shout:
"There goes John Jacob Jingelheimer
    Schmidt"
Dah, dah, dah, dah, dah, dah, dah. . . .
(*Repeat, softer each time, until no sound can
    be heard.*)

DO YOUR EARS HANG LOW

Do your ears hang low, do they wobble
    to and fro?
Can you tie them in a knot?
Can you tie them in a bow?
Can you throw them over your shoulder,
    like a continental soldier?
Do your ears hang low?

BE KIND TO YOUR WEB-FOOTED FRIENDS

(*Tune: "Stars and Stripes Forever"*)
Be kind to your web-footed friends,
For a duck may be somebody's mother.
Be kind to your friends in the swamp,
Where the weather's always damp.
You may think that this is the end. . . .
(*spoken*) WELL, IT IS!

NOW RUN ALONG HOME

Now run along home and jump
    into bed;
Say your prayers and cover
    your head.
The very same thing I say
    unto you
"You dream of me and
    I'll dream of you."

Chapter 4

BUG JUICE, MYSTERY MEAT & MEAL TICKETS

It couldn't possibly have been as awful as we made it out to be, but that never stopped us from whining to one another about the food. And it certainly didn't keep us from complaining to our parents, who might take pity on us and send a care package. (The real coup? A box of contraband candy, which provided sugar *and* popularity points.)

At most camps, certain days promised favorite menus or the horror of a particularly vile dish. At Kear-Sarge, an all-white lunch, featuring boiled potatoes, cottage cheese, sour cream, and sticky buns, was a favorite, while mystery meat, the stringy, weird stuff you couldn't positively identify, meant that most of us would be eating cold cereal for dinner. And one day a week, usually trip day, we got

NOKOMIS

bagged meals composed of sandwiches made with odd-colored roast beef or sardines and lettuce on white bread, and maybe a small, hard apple like the ones we fed to the horses. Nothing compared with parents' visiting weekend, however, which featured a memories-are-made-of-this steak platter, including curly-q fries and supplemented by a real Coke.

Two or three times a week, campers could gain entrance to the dining room only with a meal ticket, otherwise known as a letter home. Even if it was just a postcard, you had to write to your parents; apparently the camp directors thought they would want to know that we hadn't drowned or been bitten by a snake. A lot of parents received envelopes stuffed with paper that said "THIS IS A MEAL TICKET," but sometimes we did write about how much the summer meant or which counselor we hated at the moment or what needed to be sent up immediately.

Of course, we never gave any thought at all to whether our parents wanted to write to us. We expected mail from them—it was our birthright—which made daily mail call either devastating or thrilling (three letters! a package!).

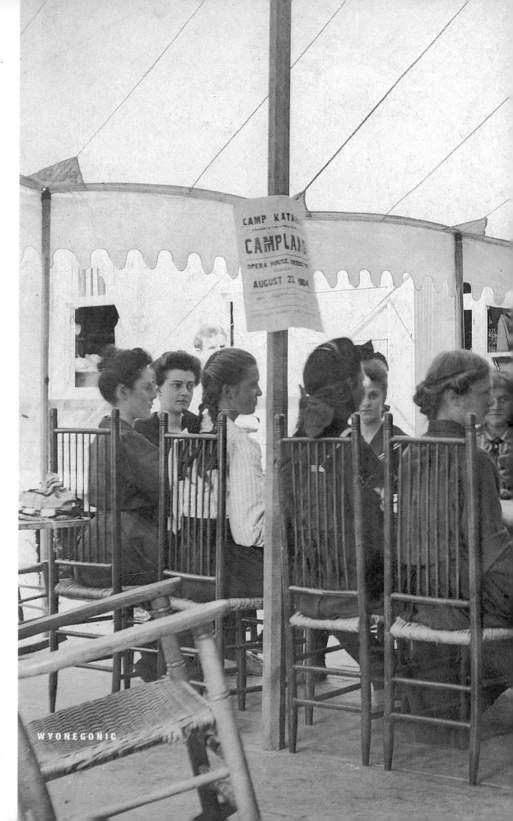

WYONEGONIC

Waldemar, 1929

Dearest, darling Mumsy,
I hope you don't feel that camp has done me no good for it has. The greatest thing I've learned is to love and appreciate home. Then I've learned to shoot a gun, row a canoe better, swim better and I am not afraid of horses. I have learned to drink milk and I can eat a little spinach.

Lots and lot of love to all, most for yourself,

Elizabeth

Mystic, 1958

Dear Folks,
I am having a wonderful time. We are starting activities on Thursday, I hope. Tuesday was thrilling. Suddenly a bell began to ring. Everybody was running all around and I discovered it was the lunch bell. (morning, noon, night bell)

In the afternoon from 2:00 to 3:30 we have to sleep and no talking or it's a check against you. Also I am a Tonk and I love it and am proud of it. I fell in love with Tonk Hill which the K's don't know about and the Tonks don't know about their hill and we have songs and rules we can't tell.

On Tuesday afternoon Jane, our counselor, was sleeping and these men were bringing in trunks. One man lifted Jane's bed real high and let it go and Jane woke up in the air.

My sister, Cinda, is not a Tonk. She is a K. Tonka is red and the K's are blue. They have white caps with red or blue which says Camp Mystic. The colors stand for the tribe.

Also they, the store, have red and also blue flashlights for the tribe fires so you can see where you are going. Tuesday night I went on Tonk Hill. After a while a girl saw a scorpine and was killed. On the K's hill some girls ran into a taranchler, those spiders that can kill people. I bought a hat, the kind I was telling you about, also a flashlight and a bathing cap that they make you wear. I have to go to sleep now. It's time, 2:00 P.M.

Sincerely,

Pam Perry

TUNA RABBIT SPAGHETTI CASSEROLE

1 ¼ pounds butter or margarine
1 ¼ pounds flour
2 tablespoons dry mustard
2 ½ tablespoons salt
1 tablespoon black pepper
2 ½ gallons hot milk
⅓ cup Worcestershire sauce
7 pounds grated sharp cheese
8 ¾ pounds flaked tuna fish
5–6 pounds spaghetti

1. Melt butter; combine with flour, mustard, salt, and pepper to make a smooth paste.

2. Stir into hot milk, beating until blended. Cook until thickened, stirring frequently. Add Worcestershire sauce and cheese, stirring until cheese is melted. Stir in tuna.

3. Cook spaghetti in boiling salted water only until tender. Drain, rinse, and drain again.

4. Place half-cupfuls of hot spaghetti in greased individual casseroles. Cover with tuna cheese sauce.

5. Bake in moderate oven (350°–370°) about 15 minutes or until thoroughly heated. Sprinkle with paprika or finely chopped parsley just before serving.

KAMAJI

NORTHWAY LODGE

PEAS, CELERY & CHEESE SALAD

13 ½ pounds cooked peas
12 ½ ounces finely chopped onions
6 ¼ pounds diced cheese
6 pounds diced celery
1 ½ pounds finely cut green pepper
2 ½ ounces salt
½ cup lemon juice
1 ½ quarts mayonnaise

1. Place peas, onion, cheese, celery, green pepper, and salt in a large mixing bowl.

2. Mix lemon juice and mayonnaise; pour over salad ingredients. Mix lightly together.

3. Serve in crisp lettuce cups.

"One of my bunkmates, Mitzi Green, said she loved hamburgers and could eat a dozen of them. So we challenged her, and sure enough, she ate twelve. Then she spent all of rest hour throwing up."

—Alice Fink Tanney, *Berkshire Hills, 1933–34*

TAPAWINGO

FERNWOOD

BUG JUICE

Early packages of Kool-Aid (invented in 1914) featured Bugs Bunny on them—hence the term *Bug's Juice* or, more simply, *bug juice*. While purists may argue that only cherry Kool-Aid can be the basis of classic bug juice, most campers agree that Hawaiian Punch, fruit punch, or any red-colored, artificial, sugary, non-carbonated beverage can be used.

CLASSIC BUG JUICE I

Serves 100

> 10 quarts prepared fruit punch
> 10 quarts ginger ale
> Juice of 10 lemons
> 8 jars maraschino cherries
> 6 cups fresh or frozen blueberries,
>   mashed

Combine liquids. Chill well. Stir in maraschino cherries and blueberries. Serve over ice.

CLASSIC BUG JUICE II

Serves 100

> 10 envelopes strawberry-flavored drink
>   mix (Kool-Aid, Wylers, whatever)
> 10 envelopes tropical punch–flavored
>   drink mix
> 20 cups sugar
> 30 quarts water

Combine all ingredients really, really well. Put in a vat. Serve over ice.

THE OFFICIAL BUG JUICE ANTHEM

(*Tune: "On Top of Old Smokey"*)

At the camp that I went to
They gave us a drink.
We thought it was Kool-Aid
Because it was pink.

But the thing that they told us
Would've grossed out a moose.
For that great-tasting pink
   drink
Was really bug juice.

It looked fresh and fruity,
Like tasty Kool-Aid.
But the bugs that were in it
Were murdered with Raid.

We drank it by gallons,
We drank it by tons,
And the very next morning
We all had the runs.

Sooooo if you drink bug juice
And a fly drives you mad,
He's just getting even
'Cause you swallowed his dad.

"I can still taste the sickeningly sweet red 'bug juice,' the watery soup and the tough meat. But the mess hall's kitchen workers were the basketball team from a Philadelphia high school, which made being a waitress so much fun. Who cared what we ate?"

—Claire Wiener Salitsky,
Akiba, 1941, 1943–45

Sing Along

Great green globs of greasy,
    grimy gopher guts,
Mutilated monkey meat, little
    birdie's dirty feet,
French-fried eyeballs, swimming
    in a pool of barf,
And I forgot my spoon.

P-I-I-I-I-G!

A girl starts by putting her right index finger on the right side of her nose. As each girl at the table (or throughout the dining hall) realizes the game has begun, she repeats that motion. The last girl at the table (or in the dining hall) without her finger on her nose is the loser. Everyone points at her and shouts, "P-I-I-I-I-G!"

"I'd never trade those summers for anything in the world." —Susan Rifkin Karon, *Matoaka*, 1969–79

SHADOW LAKE

"**We sang after every meal and had rituals for every song.** Each song was led by a different camper, who would stand on a chair in front of the whole camp. Singing the same songs, year after year, added to our sense of belonging and closeness. We were part of something with a history that was real to us. I'm totally tone-deaf, and this was my favorite part of camp. It was the only place where I wasn't embarrassed to sing."

—Jill Pincus Madenberg,
Blue Ridge, 1979–85, 1988–89, 1991

ROBINDEL

HEART O' THE HILLS

"WE ATE **WHAT?**"

ANTS ON A LOG:
Peanut butter on a celery stick
sprinkled with raisins

APHIDS ON A LOG:
Peanut butter on a celery stick
sprinkled with sunflower seeds

COW PIES:
Chocolate pudding with slivered
almonds or coconut sprinkles
(maggots)

**FLY-IN-THE-BATTER
PUDDING:**
Vanilla pudding with raisins

GNATS ON A LOG:
Peanut butter on a celery stick
sprinkled with currants

TUNA WIGGLE:
Tuna fish baked with noodles,
canned peas and Campbell's
mushroom soup

WALDEMAR

Birthday Songs

Kings and Queens and Princes, too,
Wish the best of luck to you.
So wish day, wash day,
What'd ya say, BIRTHDAY!
Happy birthday to you.

(*Tune: "Nut-Brown Maiden"*)
Dear (*name of birthday girl*), our
 hearts to you (*cover heart with
 right hand*),
Our hands to you (*extend right hand
 toward birthday girl*).
Dear (*name of birthday girl*), our
 hearts and hands to you (*cover
 heart with right hand and pull
 away with circular motion directed
 toward birthday girl*).
We pledge ourselves to your success.
Our love for you will ne'er grow less.
Dear (*name of birthday girl*), our
 hearts and hands to you (*cover
 heart with right hand, then extend
 right hand with circular motion
 toward birthday girl*).

TAPAWINGO

ALOHA

"**We were fifteen-year-old aides,** regular campers with a few extra privileges, the night we raided the kitchen and devoured an entire cake. Raiding the kitchen for ice-cream bars was fairly common; disposing of a homemade chocolate cake, which was clearly for someone's birthday, was not. The next day Willie, our camp director, announced there was no cake for our beloved counselor Carol's birthday because some selfish and inconsiderate persons had raided the kitchen. Willie spoke so quietly and sincerely that we all started crying. We were very contrite and forgiven by both Carol and Willie."

—Deborah Parker Gibbs, *Green Cove, 1968–79*

WYONEGONIC

"**We thought our director was very strict,** because we had to stand and wait for everyone to arrive at the table before we could sit down and elbows were not allowed on the table while we were eating. She thought we shouldn't speak about sex, politics, or religion, as these were subjects that create friction between people. Talking about sex was her one rule we didn't abide."

—Barbara Hartz Habermann,
Owaissa, 1956–65

FLEUR-DE-LIS

PURITY LOYALTY

SERVICE

WYONEGONIC

"I learned to eat just about everything because each camper was allowed only two dislikes. Mine were oatmeal and cream of wheat."

—Arlene Resnick Mendell, *Birch Knoll*, 1951–55

Point O' Pines, 1970
July 11

Dear Mom and Dad,
Hi! How are you? I've got a sore throat and stomachache. I am trying out for a lead in the play after rest hour. I hope my throat will clear up. There was a prowler around the camp. But now Hoby has put guards at the main entrance. We had a cookout. They ran out of salad, and the hamburgers and hot dogs weren't good. Also, the dessert was brownies with NUTS! Sailing was really great. It was very windy and I was out by myself.
Love,
Hillary

July 18

Dear Mommy and Daddy,
Hi! How are you? Last night was free night and Inter-A's could go skiing so of course I went. I skied double with Carrie Morrow. I fell after a long ride but I was lucky I fell for two reasons. One was because I had a pain in my back because the boat was going too slowly. And second, there were 3 or 4 boats which were driven by maniacs. They were trying to collide with each other and dodge each other. Ann (the driver of our boat) had to stop short because of the maniacs. Right now we're getting a lecture from our counselors. It started with stealing gum. That's why I asked for gum. I didn't steal any gum.
I miss you and love you.
Liz
PS Please tell Hil to let me use her guitar.

July 21

Dear Mom and Dad,
Hi! How are you? I need ponytail holders desperately. I went riding today. I don't know whether or not I want to quit. I'm going to ride for you on Parents Visiting Day. I hope I get to canter. A girl fell off the horse but she didn't hurt herself badly. Somebody said that Hil and me got a package from you but they were wrong.
Miss you.
Love,
Liz

August 1

Dear Mommy and Daddy,
Hi! How are you? I want to go home. I'm VERY homesick. Please don't be angry at me for having "lost" the baret, gum and dimes. The weather is raining. I WANT TO GO HOME.
Love,
Liz
PS Everyone in the bunk hates me except Ellen.

August 12

Dear Mommy and Daddy,
I moved in to my new bunk and am sleeping on the top of a bunk bed. Please make an appointment for me for a new haircut. I heard that your hair will only grow if the hair is even.
Luv,
Liz

TAPAWINGO

WALDEN

ALOHA

ILLAHEE

ARCADIA

ILLAHEE

"What I liked best was that I fit in."

—Barbara Hartz Haberman, *Owaissa, 1956–65*

GIRL SCOUT CAMP

MATAPANI (AT TAKAJO)

Chapter 5

DANCES WITH WOLVES

First there was camp. And then there were camp socials, where all of a sudden it mattered how you looked. How everyone else looked mattered, too. This was one time when you didn't want to be part of a team. At a camp social, each girl was too busy looking out for herself.

Some girls planned for the dances all summer, but most of us, if pushed, would have admitted that socials felt like an intrusion. Which is not to suggest that we didn't talk about boys or get letters from them. But we had a better time dreaming about them than having them around. The week of a social, three days were ruined. The day before the dance, the shower house was mobbed. The day of the dance, no one went to activities; time had to be spent with hair curlers, mascara, and lip gloss. The day after the social was all about the debriefing.

From most reports, rec halls and lodges all over America witnessed the same scene social after social, decade after decade: girls on one side, boys on the other, and counselors trying everything, short of cash payments, to get the two sides to mingle. Girls had primped for hours and were all dolled up; rumors that saltpeter, the dreaded mollifier of wanton sexual lusting, had been loaded into the boys' mashed potatoes only increased the tension.

And yet everyone stood around ignoring each other for at least an hour. Eventually there would be a snowball dance, which would, couple by couple, get us all onto the dance floor. And before the night was over, while the counselors guarded the front steps of the hall, girls and boys would sneak out the backstage door for a little necking down by the waterfront. But for many, the real emotional rush came after the dance was over and the boys were gone. Then the dissection of the entire affair could begin in earnest. Now, *that* was fun.

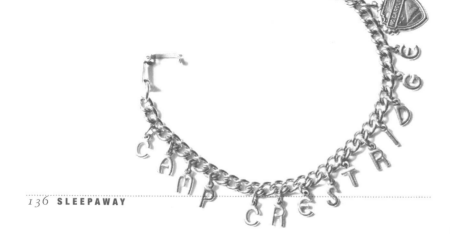

ARROWHEAD

"**I hated camp for several reasons.** I was shipped off each year for an entire month to give my *mother* a vacation. I was never given a choice or consulted. The first year I was only eight years old and a pretty shy, reclusive kid who could spend hours alone reading or playing with dolls. Interaction with kids my age was difficult. I wore glasses, was skinny and klutzy, and not the least bit athletic. My family seemed to think that camp would change all that, but it only intensified it. Everything about camp was painful and scary and embarrassing for me.

To be fair, lots of good things came from this yearly ordeal. I did learn to swim, because, honest to God, they threw me in the lake and said swim or drown. The next summer I overcame my fear of the high diving board, after three weeks of being taunted as a 'chicken.' I finally climbed that six-meter tower and jumped.

I was picked on but learned to stuff my reactions rather than express them, so the bullies moved on to girls who could provide more entertainment. Usually I was invisible; that was my best defense. That's why the group was so surprised the night of the social when the boys asked me to dance and kept asking me all evening, while the popular girls had to go ask the guys. Too bad it was the night before camp was over. Maybe I'd have gotten some mileage from it."

—Claudia Johnson Lamb Snipes,
Laughing Loon, 1954–55; Huckins, 1956–58

"Camp would have been all about boys had it been coed."

—Jeannette Foster, *Alleghany, 1979–95*

TON-A-WANDAH

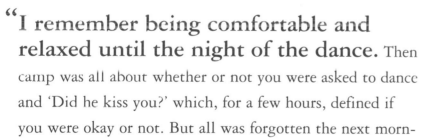

FERNWOOD

"I remember being comfortable and
relaxed until the night of the dance. Then
camp was all about whether or not you were asked to dance
and 'Did he kiss you?' which, for a few hours, defined if
you were okay or not. But all was forgotten the next morning at breakfast when they were serving our favorite crumb
cake and talk turned to teaching a cabinmate to make a
better hospital corner if we were going to improve our
inspection marks."

—Holly Louise Carlisle, *Kineowatha, 1966, 1968–74*

UNIDENTIFIED

BEST MAKE-OUT SONGS (PLUS SONGS THAT SAY SUMMER)

1920s
Stardust
More than You Know
With a Song in
    My Heart
Always

1930s
All the Things
    You Are
As Time Goes By
How Deep Is the
    Ocean
My Funny Valentine

1940s
Bewitched, Bothered
    and Bewildered
(I Love You) For
    Sentimental
    Reasons
P.S. I Love You
The Glory of Love

1950s
Pretty much anything
    by Johnny Mathis:
    Chances Are; It's
    Not for Me to Say;
    Misty; Twelfth of
    Never; Wonderful,
    Wonderful
Love Me Tender
Put Your Head on
    My Shoulder
Tennessee Waltz
In the Still of the
    Night
Til There Was You
When I Fall in Love
Where or When

1960s
Pretty much anything
    by Johnny Mathis
Can't Help Falling in
    Love
Cherish
Dedicated to the
    One I Love
Unchained Melody
And I Love Her
The Way You Look
    Tonight
You Belong to Me

1970s
Feelings
The First Time Ever
    I Saw Your Face
Muskrat Love
Love to Love You,
    Baby
Baby, I Love Your
    Way
You Needed Me
You Light Up My
    Life
Let's Get It On

1980s
Angel in the Morning
Do That to Me One
    More Time
Endless Love
You Look Wonderful
    Tonight
I Want to Know
    What Love Is
Lady
Slow Hand

1990s
I'll Make Love to You
It's All Coming Back
    to Me Now
I Will Always Love
    You (theme from
    The Bodyguard)
My Heart Will Go
    On (theme from
    Titanic)
Save the Best for Last

TODAY
God Must Have
    Spent a Little More
    Time on You
Don't Turn Off the
    Lights
Hero
Because You Loved
    Me
Breathe
Let's Make Love
For All Time

CLASSICS
Hot Fun in the
    Summertime
It Might as Well Rain
    Until September
Love Letters in the
    Sand
People Say (It's Just a
    Summer Romance)
Remember (Walkin'
    in the Sand)
Sealed with a Kiss
See You in September
Summer Wind
Summertime Blues
Under the Boardwalk
Up on the Roof
Wonderful Summer
(Itsy-Bitsy Teeny-
    Weeny) Yellow
    Polka Dot Bikini
Yesterday's Gone

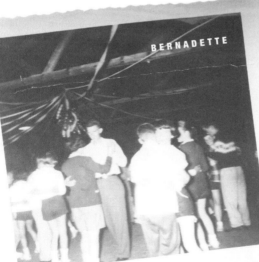

BERNADETTE

WALDEN

"**The summer I was thirteen,** I was fond of a boy from Camp Cedar. During one of our socials we decided to get friendly behind the rec hall. This was my first French kiss—and he had such bad breath! Anyway, next thing we knew, his van was driving out of camp and there was no way he could run to catch it. He had to call his director and arrange to have someone come back to pick him up. I didn't get in trouble, but my bunkmates razzed me for days. They thought he must be quite a loser if no one at his camp noticed he was missing."

—Davida Sherman Dinerman, *Matoaka, 1974–83*

🍂

"**While it's true that many a camper had her first kiss** on the steps of the rec hall, there were times when the staff would forget that we were supposed to be chaperoning, as we too were enjoying kissing on the rec hall steps."

—Susan Tomaselli Marcoux,
Notre Dame, 1965–68; Bernadette, 1969–71
(director, 1998–present)

"The older girls would come to our bunk before the dances to borrow our shorts because our shorts would be tighter on them."

—Gail Seligman Schechter, *Matoaka*, 1967–73

ILLAHEE

WALDEMAR

"The afternoon before one of our dances, when I was fourteen, I got my period and an older friend taught me how to use a tampon. I inserted it and waddled around for an hour. When I told this to my friend, she realized I'd left the applicator in."

—Andrea Brown, *Mataponi, 1960–68*

"There were some socials where the boys were fast, and we liked those camps a lot. But our counselors were always sent out on patrol to find us so you couldn't get away with much."

—Joan "Bubbles" MacFarlane Jost, *Alleghany, 1948–49, 1952–55, 1958, 1961, 1987–2001*

RUNOIA

"The rule was, there had to be six inches between you and the boy. Our camp owner actually brought a ruler with her."

—Barbara Hartz Haberman, *Owaissa*, 1956–65

WALDEMAR

"They actually paired us up by size.
They would call out two names, and a girl from one side and a boy from the other would meet in the middle, with all eyes on them. I clearly remember the feelings of excitement and dread as my name was called and then seeing what my partner looked like. I think we mostly looked forward to these socials. But many of the older girls and certainly the counselors thought of them as an interference in the camp routine."

—Ginger Saskin Boockvar, *Lenore, 1950–56*

THE VEGA PROMISE

THE MOST EXCITING THING A GIRL WILL FIND
AT VEGA IS HERSELF.

KEYSTONE

What's the Story with Saltpeter?

"**Contrary to legend, potassium nitrate (KNO_3), more commonly employed as** an ingredient in gunpowder, has no therapeutic value as an anaphrodisiac.

Still, when you look at what the stuff does do, you can see where the idea got started. Saltpeter can cause relaxation of involuntary muscle fiber (for which reason it's used to treat asthma) and it's occasionally prescribed to lower body temperature in cases of fever. From there it's not much of a leap to think that 'niter,' as it was called in the old days, might cure 'sexual fever,' and in fact a few doctors urged it for that purpose centuries ago.

The idea wasn't taken too seriously, but apparently sailors in the British navy leapt to conclusions when they learned that potassium nitrate was being used to preserve the meat used aboard their ships. Ever since, the inmates of almost any large all-male institution, ranging from boarding schools to the army, have been convinced that the higher-ups were slipping the stuff into the mashed potatoes (or whatever) to cool the jets of the rank and file.

The truth is, even the most tyrannical general wouldn't inflict the stuff on his men if he expected them to be of any use—too many side effects. Among other things, potassium nitrate can cause gastroenteritis (violent stomachache), high blood pressure, anemia, kidney disease, and general weakness and torpor. It also has an alarmingly depressive effect on the heart. Too strong a dose and not only would a guy not be able to get it up, chances are he wouldn't be able to get up, period."

—Cecil Adams,
Chicago Reader (1994)

COUCHICHING

"**Boys were an alien species to me,** so as I got older, and the pressure to be popular with them at school increased, I was thrilled to be going to a girls' camp. At home my attractiveness was offset by extreme shyness and did me little good in the boy department. But at camp dances success hinged largely on appearance; if you were cute, you got asked to dance. For the first time in my life, I was the belle of the ball and had an opportunity to feel attractive and socially successful. My first kiss and my first make-out session were both at camp socials."

—Andrea Brown, *Mataponi, 1960–68*

> "One summer I kept a diary, and my favorite entry is still: 'Had a dance with Camp Robin Hood last night. Some jerk tried to feel up Isabelle. Yuck.'"
>
> —Marcelle Harrison, *Kear-Sarge*, 1947–59

ARROWHEAD

Awanee, 1941

Dear Mom and Dad,
I have to write a long letter because I have something I must tell you. Last night we had our first dance with T.L. and what a dance it was. The first fellow I danced with was up to my chin and really was a goon. He said to me, quote, "I don't know how to dance. I'm making up my own steps. If you can follow me good, if you can't, it's too bad." The second was better. He was very nice and came from Montreal. Then the boys were alright until the next to the last dance. I was dancing with a girl when this boy cuts in. And what a boy, wow. He was the best dancer there and everyone wanted to dance with him. I had a wonderful time and I danced with him the last dance too. When we had to leave, he said that he hoped he'd see me again soon. So do I. Well, have to go to lunch.

—Babe

Danbee
7/28/92

We had a dance with Winadu and someone really, really likes me there. His name is Phillip. We slow danced and fast danced. We had a pool party at Winadu with me, Phillip, Sahar, Carly, Shannon and Carly's cousin. Boys against girls! Girls won. He is ten. He realllyyyy likes ME! I like HIM! Kind of.

Love,
Jessica

8/5/92

Dear Mom and Dad,
I just found out that Phillip dropped me. RATS! I did like him! I know this is a very, very, very, very short letter. But I have to go.

Love,
Jessica

7/93

Dear Mom and Dad,
Phillip is back! I love you and miss you. Write me.

Love,
Jessica

NATARSWI

"At O-Tahn-Agon, we had socials with Camp Mohawk. After the boys arrived at our camp, or we arrived at theirs, they would sing their camp song: 'Oh, we're the boys from Camp Mohawk and we cannot be beat . . .' It was a typical camp song, describing Camp Mohawk's greatness and the boys' athletic prowess, leadership, and all-around remarkableness. The last line of the song was particularly endearing: 'And who the hell are you?' One year, one of our girls created a parody:

> Oh, we're the girls from OTA
> And we cannot be beat.
> We never wash our hands, our face;
> We never wash our feet.
> We have BO, we have bad breath;
> We have our periods, too.
> Oh, we're the girls from OTA,
> And who the hell are you?

We practiced that song and sang it with gusto—until the boys arrived. I don't remember whether we chose not to sing it or if someone wiser made that decision for us."

—Alice Jeanne Glick Meshbane,
O-Tahn-Agon, 1965–68, 1971–72

Chapter 6

TRADITION, RITUAL & GETTING INTO TROUBLE

UNIDENTIFIED

Camp days had a rhythm, a reassuring cadence that remained familiar from year to year. We would rise at the same time every day, have meals and mail call at the same time; general swim, rest hour, and snack were always at the same time. Yet we went from activity to activity without ever knowing what time it actually was. Instead, our momentum came from our elevation of everything to the status of ritual: the way we cleaned our bunk, the way we jumped into the water for swimming, the rhymes we chanted for encouragement. We embraced tradition—some of which we created, a lot of which we inherited. Or, at least we embraced tradition and ritual most of the time.

Every August the hospital in New London, New Hampshire, held a fund-raising fair on the village green, with a parade on Main Street. Local merchants each chose a member of their shop or office to nominate as Miss New London Hospital Day and then went about raising money on her behalf. In keeping with the spirit of community, Camp Kear-Sarge always had a candidate; our job was to hit up our parents for contributions on visiting weekend. We did our best, but since the most money raised determined who wore the crown, our nominee never won.

The summer I was fourteen, no one in Senior Circle wanted to be the Kear-Sarge contestant. Forget tradition, we said; we refused to participate. Within hours the camp director had sent her response. *Every* girl in Senior Circle would try out during a pageant that would be Saturday night's entertainment, and there would be three categories of competition: talent, evening gown (a.k.a. draped bedsheets), and bathing suit. Pandemonium, hysteria, and craziness reigned for the next two days as thirty-three girls practiced wrapping themselves in bedding while identifying a performable talent. I sought advice from Janet Lefkowitz, the head of the waterfront, who I felt had shown unmatchable insight and wisdom when she recommended that my best friend, Lois DeVita, recite Kipling's "If."

WYONEGONIC

TON-A-WANDAH

TON-A-WANDAH

Janet did not disappoint me. Although I was by no means fleet of foot, Janet concluded that I should tap-dance, with cane and top hat, to "Tea for Two." She even choreographed my routine, which had me bouncing across the stage with footwork that featured one strand of steps repeated over and over. If I was going right, it was right foot brush forward and then cross over the left foot, brush right again and then scamper, scamper, scamper to the right in a sort of jerky grapevine. Repeat. Going left was exactly the same but in reverse. I knew this was silly, but I had no fear. I could not fail. I was going to tap my heart out.

At some point the bathing suit competition was dropped, to be used only as a tiebreaker, and Saturday night turned out to be a rollicking affair. At the end, Kear-Sarge had a Miss New London Hospital Day nominee, but more importantly, the tradition had been preserved—reshaped and made more meaningful.

Now, forty years later, I appreciate the artful delibera-tion of Rhoda's edict. Though she embraced a philosophy of benign neglect (she watched us like a hawk but never hovered), her primary goal was to make us realize that nobody failed at her camp; everybody was good at some-thing. But you had to try: how else could you learn that if you couldn't do this, you could do that? And that if you couldn't do that today, you could try it tomorrow?

Believing it was safe to try anything was the crucial underpinning of our trips away from camp.

Sleeping out under the stars was memorable, but meals don't get made and tents don't go up by themselves. After paddling our canoes for hours we would have to make camp and cook dinner, before we could even get to the ghost stories. We weren't always sensitive to the beauty of our surroundings—I remember one horrible night the last summer I was a camper, when we spent a mindless evening stripping bark off a grove of spectacularly beautiful birch trees—but we always saw the magic in our weekly campfires.

All week I longed for Sunday night, when light and shade would meet in the harmony of the campfire circle. As evening shadows fell and the moon started to rise, reflected brilliantly on the lake, 125 girls would become more silent and still than seemed possible, waiting for that week's chosen group to rise and speak about noble aspirations, ideals, and solidarity. Then, as flames became embers, we'd sing beautiful and hopeful songs of peace and oneness. This coming together in speech and song and friendship was the only place I've ever found where I could comfortably express a reverence for things of the spirit.

"The friends I made at camp are peop[le] on my life." —Mary Milne Marshall, *Glen Bernard, 1978–99*

ARROWHEAD

who have had the greatest impact

PEACE, I ASK OF THEE, O RIVER

Peace, I ask of thee, O River,
Peace, peace, peace.
When I learn to live serenely,
   cares will cease.
From the hills I gather courage,
Visions of the days to be.
Strength to lead and strength
   to follow
All are given unto me.
Peace, I ask of thee, O River,
Peace, peace, peace.

TELL ME WHY

Tell me why the stars do shine,
Tell me why the ivy twines,
Tell me why the sky's so blue,
And I will tell you just why
   I love you.

Because God made the stars to
   shine
Because God made the ivy twine
Because God made the skies so
   blue
Because God made you is why
   I love you.

FATHER TIME

Father time is a crafty man and
   he's set in his ways.
And we know that we never can
   make him bring back past
   days.
So campers, while we are here,
   let's be friends firm and true.
We'll have a gay time, a happy
   playtime,
'Cause we all love to play with
   you.

TAPS

Day is done, gone the sun
From the lakes, from the hills,
   from the sky.
All is well, safely rest.
God is nigh.

Fading light dims the sight
And a star gems the sky, gleam
   ing bright.
From afar, drawing nigh,
Falls the night.

Thanks and praise for our days
'Neath the sun, 'neath the stars,
   'neath the sky.
As we go, this we know,
God is nigh.

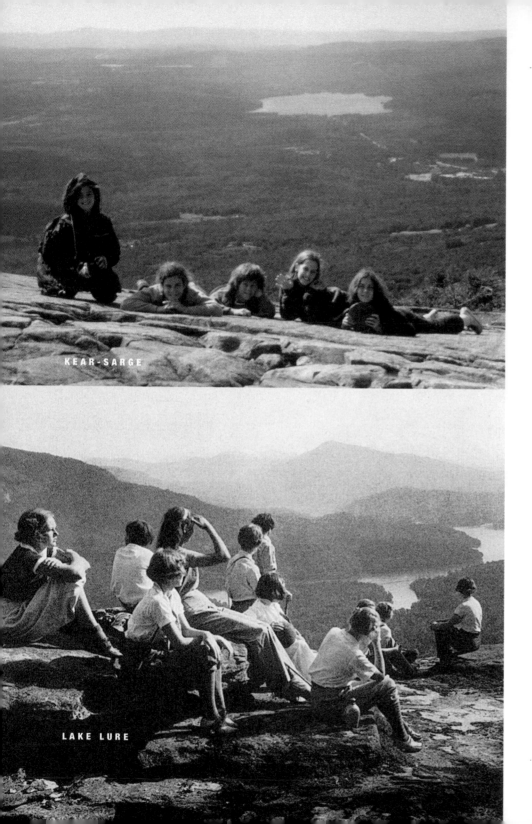

KEAR-SARGE

LAKE LURE

"**Our trip to the White Mountains was terrifying.** We never exercised or stretched or conditioned ourselves. We would play an hour of basketball and then make a lanyard. Nonetheless, one morning we shipped off to climb Mt. Washington.

Our guide, who must have been from Switzerland, had on short shorts and a heavy backpack. He basically ran up the mountain. None of us had on the right shoes or the right clothes, and we had zero endurance. Somehow we made it to the top and our rustic sleeping accommodation at Lake of the Clouds Inn. Once we were informed that we'd be sleeping dormitory style, with strangers, in triple-decker beds, no one closed an eye. In the morning as we charged outside in our little shorts and T-shirts, only to discover it had snowed, our group of Sarah Bernhardts thought, 'FROSTBITE! WE'RE DEAD!'

We made it down without incident, but the stories of our misery, circulated by us for the rest of that summer and then for years to come, were early Stephen King. By the time we finished, it sounded as though we'd been through a trek on Kilimanjaro."

—Vickie Lieberman Desatnick,
Kear-Sarge, 1960, 1962–70

RUNOIA

ILLAHEE

CAMP SIGHTS

mist rising above the glassy
smooth surface of the lake

starry nights

everyone walking around
with arms around one
another's shoulders

swimming staff with zinc
oxide on their noses

CAMP SMELLS

pine trees

dining hall food

the rec hall

green soap

damp sleeping bags

campfire smoke

the arts-and-crafts lodge

Listerine in the infirmary

toasted marshmallows

balsam

insect repellent

mildew

Prell shampoo

fresh laundry with starch

gasoline from the water-
skiing boat

wet concrete in the shower

wool blankets

Coppertone suntan lotion

"**Our canoe trip up the Crooked River was hilarious.** We spread our ponchos in hollows on the riverbank, but that evening there was a terrific rainstorm and many of the girls got soaked. Those of us who had stayed dry each took a camper into our ponchos, which were only supposed to hold one person. Much giggling as we tried to turn over! Another item: some of the girls had fun sliding down the sand bank, until they wore out the bottoms of their bathing suits."

—Dorothy Bruegger Mausolff, *Wohelo*, 1917–18

"**I was sixteen, and we were on the annual Crooked River trip** when a horrible lightning and rain storm sprang up. There was no shelter nearby, and we were paddling metal canoes. Seeing the desperate situation, my friend Susan and I took all the drenched, shivering campers out of their canoes and huddled as a group under a tarp. These ten little blue-lipped campers were scared and bordering on hypothermia, so we started singing 'You Are My Sunshine' at the top of our lungs.

After you've endured rain, cold, and fatigue with someone who has proved herself a good sport, you're more likely to listen, with an open mind, to her opinion."

—Merry Wells Logan, *Wohelo*, 1979–85

Sit in a circle, Indian style, with knees touching. Sing the song below, starting with your hands on your knees. Place your right hand on the knee of the girl to your right and your left hand on the knee of the girl to your left; hands back on own knees. Cross your arms so your right hand is on your left knee and your left hand is on your right knee; hands back on own knees. Place your right hand on the knee of the girl to your right and your left hand on the knee of the girl to your left; hands back on own knees.

Repeat the song with the same hand motions, singing faster and faster until it rains—or you fall over laughing.

A-woonie-woonie-kai-i-woonie.
A-woonie-woonie-kai-i-woonie.
Ai-ai-ai-icky-ai-kai-ainu.
Ai-yi-yi-yippie-yi-ki-ainu,
A-woo, a-woo, a-woonie-keechi.

ALTERNATE MOTIONS

Sing the song three times, making the following hand motions in time with the four beats of each line: 1) slap thighs; clap hands; slap thighs, clap hands; 2) slap own thighs on first two beats; slap thighs of neighbor to right on third and fourth beats (alternate slapping thighs of right and left neighbors); 3) with right arm straight out at shoulder, touch right wrist with left hand; touch top of right elbow; touch right shoulder; cross right arm over left (alternate with left arm).

UNIDENTIFIED

CAMP SOUNDS

loons on the lake

the wind in pine trees

listening to a storm at
night in a tent

absolute calm of the lake
before flag raising

the morning wake-up
bell, bugle, or foghorn

plates being moved in
the dining hall

wavelets lapping on the
shore

music coming from the
rec hall

the crunch of dried pine
needles underfoot

tennis balls being hit

girls giggling

whistles being blown

SINGING!

the clank of a bunk
screen door slamming

mosquitoes buzzing your
ear as you're falling
asleep

taps

whispering during
rest hour and after lights
out

owls

the clang of the chain on
the flagpole

WOHELO

ILLAHEE

"I recall being on a backpacking trip, in the Shining Rock Wilderness of western North Carolina, with a trip leader whose philosophy was: 'If you're not helping, then go away and play.' There were six of us who had become close friends that summer, and none of the six was listed on the evening's chore chart, so we set off into the woods.

We located a spot surrounded almost completely by rhododendron where we could solve the world's problems. I remember exactly what this location looked like, smelled like and felt like, probably because the moment is so representative of my camp experience. We were able to enjoy great fellowship, independent from the larger group (thanks to our rhododendron curtain), yet we felt safe and protected, close to the larger group and our counselors.

But, make no mistake, girls will be girls and a camp full of females was not exempt from the cliquishness that occurs in a school setting. And while I was generally accepted for who I was, every now and then I'd find 'who I was' was outside the circle."

—Carole Hicks Hilderbran, *Illahee, 1975–88*

ILLAHEE SLOGAN

IT'S MORE THAN A PLACE; IT'S A FEELING.

WINONA

Wohelo, 1926

Dear Family—

Everyone get settled comfortably and be prepared for a lengthy epistle, for I have just oodles and oodles and oodles to write about. First—I have been around the lake! It was the most wonderful three days I have ever lived through, and I never had a better time; so I shall begin at the beginning and tell it all in detail. Then, next winter when some of the smaller incidents have left my mind, all I will have to do is refer to this letter for a complete record.

There were eighteen of us in the crowd—Tinkie included. Tommie Pierce drove Bunco, the Ford truck, and any who were tired or blistered took turns riding with her. We left camp at nine o'clock Wednesday morning and walked steadily till about eleven, when we stopped at Songo Locks for some ice cream and a drink. We had easily swung into a good pace and had covered about eight miles.

We had lunch about two hours later, some five miles this side of North Sebago. Gypsy brew, sandwiches, fruit and cake make up all our lunches, and you can't realize just how cooling and refreshing that combination is. While we had a short rest hour, Tommie drove ahead with the truck and dumped the ponchos at the place where we would camp that night—two miles the other side of North Sebago.

Thursday we hiked about sixteen miles and landed in Sebago Lake Station around five. Several of us had haircuts, we bought out the ice cream, and then Bunco drove us all to Grey's just outside the village.

Friday morning we woke up bright and early, and after consuming nineteen blueberry pancakes apiece, with crispy bacon and eggs, we rolled our ponchos, said good-bye to the Greys and started off once more.

Six miles to go and then camp!!

We were so happy at the thought that we fairly raced the rest of the way; and yet we could have turned around and gone straight back again around the lake.

At the top of Lewa Hill we stopped and then raced pell-mell down the hill, onto the dock, and into the water with all our clothes on. Such splashing and shouting you never heard as when eighteen of us washed away the dust and dirt of five towns in Sebago's sparkling waters blue. Thus ended our Gypsy Trip.

Love to all,
Peggy Holmes

WOHELO

WYONEGONIC

GIRLS VACATION FUND CAMP

"I adored camp for many reasons, but what I loved most was the Canadian, the ultimate ten-day canoe trip. Only the most experienced camper/canocists were chosen; I earned the privilege twice.

Paddling for hours, portaging between lakes, stopping for snacks or lunch or just to look around at the beauty that surrounded us, we'd make camp in the late afternoon. We drank out of the lakes, washed in the lakes, swam in the lakes, and listened to the echo of our voices while in the lakes. The food was always the best, because we prepared it ourselves and then sat around sharing it. Dessert was a bar of Baker's chocolate. Since there were six letters in the name *Baker's* and there were five of us, we'd each get a letter and then decide who should get the extra piece.

Setting up our tent late in the afternoon, building a fire, preparing the meal, washing the dishes, going to bed, giggling in the tent, getting up the next morning, cooking a hot breakfast, and then pushing off for another day of paddling: what more could a girl want? It was magical."

—**Barb Fearing McNair Moberg,**
Minne Wonka Lodge, 1963–69

NATARSWI

WYONEGONIC

"**We were on a canoe trip** on Sebago Lake when I woke up in the night to find there was blood everywhere on my sleeping bag. Panicky, because I was convinced some animal had bitten me, I woke everyone in the tent. It took a while for me to understand I had gotten my first period."

—**"Ellie,"** *Hiawatha, 1948–56*

"This Is My Creed"

To live each day as though I may never see the morrow come; to be strict with myself, but patient and lenient with others; to give the advantage, but never ask for it; to be kind to all, but kinder to the less fortunate; to respect all honest employment; to remember always that my life is made easier and better by the service of others, and to be grateful.

To be tolerant and never arrogant; to treat all men with equal courtesy; to be true to my own in all things; to make as much as I can of my strength and the day's opportunity; and to meet disappointment without resentment.

To be friendly and helpful whenever possible; to do without display of temper or bitterness, all that fair conduct demands; to keep my money free from cunning or the shame of a hard bargain; to govern my actions so that I may fear neither reproach nor misunderstanding, nor words of malice or envy; and to main- tain, at whatever temporary cost, my own self-respect.

This is my creed and my philosophy. I have failed it often and shall fail it many times again; but by these teachings I have lived to the best of my ability— laughed often, loved, suffered, grieved, found consolation and prospered. By friendships my life has been enriched, and the home I am building is happy.

—*Comanche vesper service of 1934, first used in the second term and now a cherished part of the Spirit of Waldemar Ceremony*

"Here you go to sleep to the sound of the wind . . ."

—Heather Brown Holleman, *Greystone, 1994–99*

GIRL SCOUT CAMP

OVERNIGHT HIKE MENUS

WIENERS STUFFED WITH CHEESE
AND WRAPPED WITH BACON,
ROASTED ON A STICK

BUTTERED BUNS

PICKLES

CARROTS

S'MORES

JUICES AND SODA

PIONEER STEW

BISCUITS MADE IN A
REFLECTOR OVEN

TOMATO SECTIONS

PEACHES

JUICES AND SODA

KAHDALEA

"I liked not feeling lazy." —Bernice Haase Luck, *Beverly, 1942–45*

KAMAJI

FERNWOOD

S'MORES

The first recipe for s'mores appeared in *Tramping and Trailing with the Girl Scouts*, published by Girl Scouts of the U.S.A. in 1927.

HOW TO MAKE A S'MORE

Serves 1

A green stick
2 marshmallows
1 graham cracker
4 squares of plain chocolate

Put the marshmallows on your stick. Toast them over the coals to a crispy, gooey, golden brown. Break the graham cracker in half. Place the chocolate on a graham cracker half, and then mush the marshmallows on top. Squish down, using the other graham cracker half. If you're lucky, the heat of the marshmallow will melt the chocolate. Eat.

CAMP CARONDOWANNA
YWCA

EATS FOR OVERNIGHTS

BEANHOLE BEANS

Serves 15

> 2 ½ pounds navy beans
> 1 ½ pounds salt pork or bacon
> 4 ½ teaspoons salt
> ½ cup sugar
> ½ cup molasses

Wash beans and soak them overnight. Next morning, parboil them until the skins split.

Drain beans and place them in a heated earthen pot with slices of pork in the center; add salt, sugar, and molasses. Cover closely and bake in a bean hole for 6 to 8 hours.

To make a beanhole: Dig a hole 1½ feet in diameter and 1½ feet deep. Line the hole with stones and keep a fire burning inside it for several hours before using it so the stones will be hot. When the beans are ready in the pot, rake out the ashes and coals and place the prepared pot in the hole; cover with hot coals. The hole should be covered with earth while the beans cook.

WYONEGONIC

WYONEGONIC

ARCADIA

SLUM GULLION
Serves 15

>   *2 cans pimientos*
>   *4 hard-boiled eggs*
>   *2 cans tuna*
>   *2 No. 2 cans peas*
>   *Salt and pepper*
>   *3 tablespoons butter or bacon fat*
>   *3 cups milk (may use evaporated or*
>   *powdered)*
>   *3 tablespoons flour*

Cut up the pimientos and eggs; combine with tuna, peas, and seasonings.

To make white sauce: Melt butter or fat and stir in flour until mixture is smooth and thick. Add milk slowly. Stir and cook until mixture takes on the consistency of cream.

Pour white sauce over tuna mixture.

Heat thoroughly in an open kettle over the fire or in a pan set before a reflector oven. If the latter method is used, sprinkle bread crumbs over the top.

CAMP
TON·A·WANDAH

"At home I was treated like a baby, but at camp people depended on me. I had responsibilities."
—Arlene Resnick Mendell, *Birch Knoll, 1951–55*

ALOHA HIVE

WALDEN

ARCADIA

"Camp was the single most important part of my growing up, and I strongly believe that, in one way or the other, everything I am I owe to camp. Our camp director was the one person in my life who believed in and encouraged me. I didn't realize it at the time, but she was my *mentor*, a word that may not have existed then."

—Jean Sack Wollan, *Birchwood, 1942–53*

ALOHA

"**On the last day of a canoe trip,** my best friend Charlotte and I decided that before we paddled across Boulder Lake, we'd stop off at a roadside/riverside restaurant for an ice-cream cone. Although this would mean breaking a camp rule, at sixteen we thought we could get away with it. As Charlotte stepped out of the canoe, observed by all the diners, the top of her bathing suit dropped to her waist. We never did get those cones."

—Betsy A. Behnke, *Manito-Wish, 1956–64*

WYONEGONIC

WOHELO

ALOHA

CLEARWATER

"One evening we sat around the camp-fire talking about fireflies and fairies. Then, in the middle of the night, we were awakened and taken out to a field where, lo and behold, there were ethereal fairies dancing around the flagpole in gauzy array. The next morning we reported the event to the whole camp. I was seven at the time, and for years afterward I was never sure about the reality, or not, of fairies. But then when I was a counselor, I found myself leaping and cavorting around the flagpole wrapped in mosquito netting with some very young campers watching, entranced."

—Nancy Marcus Harris, *Burr Oaks*, 1933, 1935, 1937–38, 1946

> "I learned that singing with female voices around a campfire is a powerful, almost magical experience." —Patricia "Trish" Richardson Mann, *Green Cove, 1968-74, 1976–80, 1986*

KICKAPOO KAMP

PRANKS

Pranks are not about being mean, or about getting hurt. They're about having fun and running a little bit wild while you're still young enough to get away with it. Pranks are about someone getting wet or messy, or about a counselor having to row out to the waterskiing dock to retrieve her cubbie, and they're at the heart of the camp experience.

I pulled off one of my favorite pranks in 1960, when I managed to appear not once but twice in the camp panorama picture. I was at first seated on the left end of the front row, but as the camera began its slow move, I raced around to the other end of the row—and got there before it did. And then there was the summer I was thirteen. Since our counselor, Becky, had never actually attended camp before, we kindly explained to her that counselors at Kear-Sarge made their campers' bed on Sundays. We thought we were golden that first Sunday until Batch, the head counselor, walked into our cabin quite unexpectedly and asked, "WHAT is going on here?" Whoops. But we didn't mind making Becky's bed for the next three days; it was all in the spirit of give-and-take.

If only I could figure out who removed every single pair of shoes from each and every bunk one night the next summer . . . I'd like to show her a little about give-and-take. That's one of the great things about having been a camper: a good prank can still get you going.

—L.S.K.

THE CLASSICS

Short-sheeting (a.k.a. frenching or pieing) a bed

Raising bras on the flagpole

Tying tent flaps from the outside

Putting a sleeping bunkmate's hand into warm water to see if she would wet her bed

Wrapping the toilet seat with plastic wrap

Smearing Vaseline on a toilet seat

Painting the mark of Zorro on each camper's forehead with gentian violet

Rowing the counselor's bed out to the raft on her day off

"If I hadn't gone to bed early, this would have been my last camp memory: Some of my friends put Nair on a sleeping girl's eyebrows 'to see what would happen.' When the girl woke up in the morning, her eyebrows were gone and, before I knew it, so were my friends. Fourteen years later, I happened to see the girl at a wedding and she was still penciling in her eyebrows."

—Ellen Blumberg Framm, *Louise, 1976–87*

"One summer we had a head counselor whose only concern was the lost-and-found. So, we took the sliding board from lower campus, hung a large sign on it that said 'LOST,' and put it on the steps of her bunk. The only way she could get out was to slide down it!"

—Bernice "Bunny" Klein Sherman, *Rhoda, 1943–44, 1958–68*

"I was able to contort my face and move my eyes in a way tht resembled a fish. This was a popular request at camp. I never imitated a fish at school."

—Alice Jeanne Glick Meshbane, *O-Tahn-Agon, 1965–68, 1971–72*

ROCKBROOK

"**The girls I went to camp with** were some of the prissiest, brattiest people I have ever met. They were determined to make others uncomfortable about being themselves. Anyone with a little individuality was made to feel awkward; one girl was always singled out. It was like junior high in a pretty environment."

—Sylvia Borenstein, *Seafarer, 1987–89, 1992*

"**I decided to sneak out of camp one night** to go say hi to a friend at the boys' camp. The moon was shining bright as I came back onto campus, and I noticed what I thought was one of the camp cats walking toward me. As it came closer, I bent down to pat it and realized there were two large white stripes running down its back. I broke into a run and landed in my cabin doorway with such a thud that the whole bunk woke up and I had to concoct a story about being at the wash house. Fortunately, no one noticed I wasn't in my pajamas."

—Elaine Knight Griffith, *Betsy Cox, 1960–69*

GREYSTONE IDEALS

Sincerity. Courage. Honesty. Kindness. Truth.

KEYSTONE

"Camp Bernadette has a long-standing tradition of pranks; it's part of our culture. We have a small, two-foot-tall statue of the Blessed Virgin Mother and she is often found in inconvenient locales. Currently she's in my living room, at home. Three of my staff took her from camp at the end of the summer and deposited her on my front lawn on Christmas Eve."

—Susan Tomaselli Marcoux,
Notre Dame, 1965–68; Bernadette, 1969–71 (director, 1998–present)

"I told the director that my cousin, from out of town, was coming to visit and that I needed permission to leave camp. The 'cousin' was actually a boy I'd met at a social and kept in touch with over a period of two years. I was busted when I didn't take my sister with me to meet him. DUH!!!"

—Debbi Ogan Fendel, *Matoaka, 1966–69*

Camp FAIR HAVEN

PINECLIFFE

HOW TO "PIE" A BED

When you make a real pie, first you roll out the crust, fold it in half, and place it with the fold in the center of the pie. Then you carefully pull the folded part over to make the whole crust. From this process comes the term *pie bed*.

How to make a pie bed: Begin by taking everything off except the bottom sheet. Leave that as is. Next, take the top sheet and tuck it in at the top as you would a bottom sheet. Then bring the bottom part of the sheet just up to the top of the bed, leaving room to pull it over the blankets. You now have a half-length of sheet into which the person will have to find room for her feet. After the top sheet is done and the blankets put on as they were before you stripped the bed, you have to be sure to do hospital corners. Remember how the person whose bed you're making had her pillow covered. That's a dead giveaway. Now run like hell and hope you have not been spotted. The hardest part is keeping the secret to yourself.

—Elizabeth "Chippy" Bassett Wolf, *Aloha Hive, 1943; Aloha, 1945, 1948–53*

"**Short-sheeting someone's bed** is always a great prank, but one fine night it was especially amusing. As we watched our tent mate struggle to get into her bed, the legs of the folding cot collapsed and the whole thing slid out of the tent, down a short hill, and into the lake. I literally peed in my pants. She was okay, by the way, but we did get into a bit of trouble for that one."

—Betsy Perry Danforth, *Kehonka, 1966–73*

"**One night after taps,** my best friend and I snuck out of our bunk to visit some senior girls. We'd only been at their tent a few minutes when we heard the night-duty counselors coming. We scrambled out the back and started running. At one point I looked behind me and my friend wasn't there, so I doubled back to find her. She had run into a clothesline, gotten tangled up in the hanging towels and bathing suits, and was lying in a heap, laughing hysterically. We were reprimanded, but the counselors couldn't help laughing, too."

—Jill Grayson Finkelstein, *Tripp Lake, 1957–63, 1965*

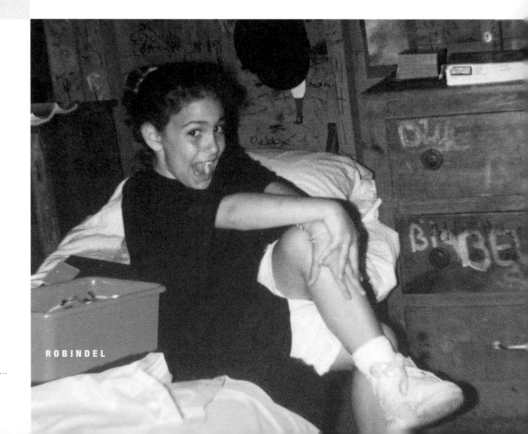

ROBINDEL

MUDJEKEEWIS

"When someone was in the shower, with a head full of lathered shampoo, we'd tell her she had a phone call, which meant she'd have to run down to the administration building on the other end of camp. So whenever you saw someone charging down the path with a soapy head of hair, you knew."

—Amy Silver Kramer, *Che-Na-Wah, 1974–88*

CLEARWATER

"Never again will I find friends like my camp friends."

—Betsy Strum Ellis, *Appalachia*, 1967, 1971–85

WALDEN

WOHELO

"**In 1958, when I was fifteen,** a group of us who had been going to camp together since we were six lived in the senior bunk. The owners had chosen to put a new counselor in with us, and we thought she was such a nerd, we nicknamed her Schmozie Rosie.

We decided to sneak out—but during the day. We traipsed through the woods and spent hours eating junk food and smoking. We heard the troops searching and calling but managed to evade them. We finally got bored, went back, climbed onto the roof of our bunk, and came down during rest hour. We lay on our beds reading and doing our nails, and when Schmozie walked in, in tears, we acted as though she had lost her mind. Needless to say, we didn't see the light of day for about two weeks.

But being seniors was the best, because that was when you'd dare to peroxide your hair. My first try was less than successful, and I tried to cover up the yellowish-green-orange streaks with brown shoe polish."

—Barbara Kaplan Kramer, *Geneva, 1950–60*

"**All my camp photos have somehow vanished,** but I still carry pictures of the love of my life, Camp Louise, in my heart."

—Vicki Campbell-McNutt, *Louise, 1945–59*

"Camp was the first place I laughed so hard I cried."

—Barbara Bell Barrett, *Greystone, 1972–78, 1983*

WYONEGONIC

"One time on Tonk Tribe Hill, a little junior camper passed gas rather loudly at a particularly quiet and serious moment. We knew that everyone had heard her, but as senior officers we were determined to control our composure. Tears were streaming down our faces and we were about to explode with laughter, but we did our best to contain ourselves. Just as we were about to recover from the 'interruption,' Jennifer whispered to me, 'How could that much noise come out of that little body?' I lost it then. So did the rest of the senior officers. Our only hope was that the younger campers thought we were grimacing and sniffling and weeping over our heartfelt love for the Tonkawa Tribe and because of the moving speeches that had been given.

Another time on Tonk Hill, we were preparing a big ceremony to kick off our Field Day theme for the tribe and we used kerosene-soaked Kotex to make flaming arrows. It seemed like a good idea at the time. But it's hard to stay solemn when you know that flaming sanitary napkins are flying through the air across the whole Tonkawa Tribe."

—Martha Maynard, *Mystic, 1972–80*

TAPAWINGO

GIRLS VACATION FUND CAMP

The Girls of Camp Lenore

"**Although Lenore, like other such enterprises, had its required quota of athletic activities—swimming and canoeing, baseball, basketball, tennis, track—it was not**

merely a place to which parents sent their young daughters during school vacations so they might live healthily outdoors and be instructed in sports. Mrs. Spectorsky's camp was a place of spiritual aspiration and dedication before it was a place for the development of our physical competences. It was an aesthetic rather than an athletic camp. Indeed, it was at Lenore that, at the age of thirteen, fourteen, fifteen, my pores open to whatever might come to me either by chance or by adult design, I first discovered this new and wider dimension of life, the dimension of art, a range of emotion and perception that had previously not been accessible to me.

Our camp day began at Lenore with morning assembly, and regularly the directress took advantage of this gathering of her young charges to remind us of what it was that distinguished

us from other summer camps for girls and in what way we were beneficiaries of this difference. It was not the body that was neglected at Mrs. Spectorsky's camp. 'Mens sana in corpore sano— a healthy mind in a healthy body,' the directress translated with even emphasis.

We were a hundred and forty campers and between thirty and forty counselors. And at least half of our counselors were chosen for their skill in dance or drama or the crafts. In addition, Mrs. Spectorsky engaged a trio of musicians—a pianist, a violinist, and a cellist—to perform for us each afternoon.

It was at these afternoon concerts provided for us by Mrs. Spectorsky's trio, all of them aspirants to professional careers, that there was confirmed in me what was undoubtedly an inborn love of music; it was sufficiently strong to have withstood even

the teachings of Professor Steinmetz. The concerts took place at five each afternoon in the assembly hall, and they were entirely devoted to classical music: Brahms and Tchaikovsky, Schubert, Dvořák, Faure. Music hour was not compulsory, but I never failed to attend. Weather permitting, I listened outdoors, sitting on the veranda floor with my back against the rough shingles. As I sat gazing toward the surrounding hills, the music would drift out to me and my heart would swell with longing. From my earliest years, longing was always my secret companion.

Mrs. Spectorsky had ruled against ballet at Lenore. She said it was against nature to bind our poor little feet in tight silk slippers and to try to raise ourselves on our toes. At Lenore we danced in Grecian tunics, barefoot and bare-legged, in the manner of Isadora Duncan. No art could be

art, said the directress, if it entailed suffering. Art was joy and love; art was transcendence.

I was the readiest of Mrs. Spectorsky's youthful adherents and I very much wanted to achieve transcendence, but I was too self-conscious to dance. I had come to Lenore with the sad knowledge that, aspiring though I might be in mind, I was sorely lacking in physical grace, and to this dispiriting self-assessment had been added the appraisal of my bunkmates. Their judgement was final. My legs were too thin and my knees too bumpy to merit careless exposure. I must find other means of participating in the pageants that were so notable a feature of our dramatic program.

Like our dance classes, our pageants took place on the lawn in front of the lodge. They were a composite of narrative and dance. Sometimes the drama counselor,

"We danced in Grecian tunics, barefoot and bare-legged."

—Diana Trilling, *Lenore*, 1918–24

WAUKELA

"You could become better, but you were unique and important as you were." —Nancy Marcus Harris, *Burr Oaks*, 1933–34, 1937–38

WE-HA-KEE

more often Mrs. Spectorsky herself, acted as narrator. Majestic, classical, the directress would stand on the steps of the lodge and with vibrant voice call upon the ancient religious mysteries to reenact themselves. 'With fruits and flowers we deck thy altars,' her wonderful contralto rang out to the surrounding hills, while to the accompaniment of this and other similarly broad-minded sentiments a dozen barefoot little dancers, virgin priestesses in the Temple of Aphrodite, disported themselves on the wide green lawn in front of the lodge. They bore baskets of crepe-paper offerings that had been fashioned for them during the previous week in our arts-and-crafts classes.

There were few opportunities to raise our artistic consciousness which the directress left unexplored. One summer, she invited Robert Frost to speak at Lenore. The poet was staying in Pittsfield, only a dozen or so miles from camp. Though not yet the

eminence that he would become, Frost was already a poet of repute. Yet it was actually not as a literary man but as a man of nature that Mrs. Spectorsky invited him to speak to us. A slithering green snake had been seen near one of the intermediate bunks, and Lenore was on the brink of panic. The visit from the local woodsman was intended to assure us that our snakes would do us no harm.

While no note was taken of conventional religion at Lenore, the directress was far from a non-believer or lacking in religious sentiment. Scornful of sects and

denominations, she had her own sacraments and was indubitably to be counted among the devout. Her immediate leanings were toward the religious teachings of the East, but in total she was a worshiper at the shrine of the immaterial. She aspired to the whole wide glorious universe of spirit.

If ever the directress's capacity for rising above the impositions of worldliness was tried, it was on parent weekends. Each summer, there were two weekends on which parents were permitted, even urged, to visit their children. For the few hours in which

they were in possession, Lenore trembled under the intrusion of this alien culture. The mothers and fathers arrived at Lenore like an invasive horde in their shiny new Packards and Pierce-Arrows, the fathers wearing plaid golf knickers and broad-patterned argyle socks, the mothers brilliant in their expensive summer outfits. Not even Mrs. Spectorsky's poise and cultivated speech could threaten the confidence of these noisy invaders—having paid for their children's summer tuition, the parents apparently felt they had bought, if only for these few hours, the right to its

lawns and lake, its assembly and mess halls.

At Monday morning assembly after a parents weekend, the directress would quietly address the daughters of the rich and noisy on how the voice and the heart were one: a hundred and forty girls were once more instructed in the difference between striving and aspiration, this ill-marked crossroads at which the directress took up her pedagogic post. Gravely she explained to us that, while there was much that was laudable in being a good swimmer or tennis player, at Lenore the goal was a willing rather than a winning. Better to play the game poorly or run the race in which we suffered defeat than not to extend ourselves, not to try. Within each of us, she summed up, was an inner gleam that must guide us.

For all the directress's tireless teaching—'Girls, be kind to one another'—kindness was often in short supply among us, especially among the older girls. How cruelly we teased the girl in the next senior bunk because,

unlike the rest of us, she had not yet begun to menstruate! During one of my own menstrual periods, Mimi Pomeroy, who was the camp's fat girl and my enemy, said to me threateningly, 'I'll kick you and a pound will flow!' Without comprehending what the threat could mean, I was much troubled by its menace. Even now it disturbs me to recall it.

As a counselor, I returned to Lenore. Then Lionel and I were married, and I didn't again see Lenore or its directress until more than a decade had passed. In my mid-thirties, a settled married woman, I was driving in New England with Lionel when all at once it came to me that we were in the vicinity of my old camp. I burst out, 'Let's go to Lenore!'

Only much later, when we were driving away from camp and I was trying, not very suc-

FARNSWORTH

cessfully, to still my pain and anger at the scant notice that Mrs. Spectorsky had taken of me, did I realize that I had of course invited just such rejection by dropping in at Lenore this unexpectedly. Mrs. Spectorsky suffered with grace the intrusion of the parents on those weekends; for the rest of the summer, the seclusion and routine of Lenore must not be interrupted. I was not part of this routine. I had once been part of Lenore,

but I no longer shared in it. Now it belonged to other girls, little girls like the Bluebirds and bigger girls as well, edging toward womanhood, making their way through the wilderness of their ignorance and their desires. I was no longer part of Mrs. Spectorsky's history as she was part of mine."

—Diana Trilling,
Lenore, 1918–24

RED-LETTER DAYS

SUNDAY	MONDAY	TUESDAY	WEDNESDAY	THURSDAY	FRIDAY	SATURDAY
JULY 6 CAMPFIRE	**7** MOVIE NIGHT	**8** COUNSELOR HUNT	**9** BACKWARDS DAY	**10** SUNAPEE CANOE TRIP →	**11**	**12**
13 CAMPFIRE	**14** DANCE WITH CAMP SAMOSET	**15** SWIM MEET	**16** CAMP PHOTOS	**17** NEW LONDON PLAYERS **BRIGADOON**	**18** CAMPER-COUNSELOR DAY	**19** OPERETTA BY JUNIOR CAMPERS
20 CAMPFIRE	**21** MYSTERY BUS RIDE	**22** CLIMB & SLEEP OVERNIGHT ON → MT. WASHINGTON	**23**	**24** INTERCAMP COMPETITION WITH CAMP ROBINDEL	**25** COSTUME BALL	**26** PARENTS VISITING WEEKEND
27 CAMPFIRE	**28** MOVIE NIGHT	**29** ALL-CAMP BIRTHDAY PARTY	**30** SWIM MEET	**31** THE COUNSELOR SHOW	**AUGUST 1** DANCE & OVERNIGHT AT CAMP ROBIN HOOD	**2** SENIOR SHOW **OLIVER**
3 CAMPFIRE	**4** CAMPER vs. COUNSELOR SOFTBALL GAME	**5** WATER CARNIVAL	**6** TALENT SHOW	**7** PROGRESSIVE DINNER	**8** HOOTENANNY	**9** PICKING BLUEBERRIES FOR SUNDAY PIE

"Now when I go to visit camp, if there's anything I want to complain about it's that they've changed some minute detail about one of my beloved traditions. I immediately find myself thinking, 'There goes camp. They're going to ruin it.'"

—Joanne Newbold, *Newfound, 1964–68*

WYONEGONIC

"**Mrs. S. was the director** of Camp Notre Dame, a small, Catholic girls' camp in Munsonville, New Hampshire, that I adored attending for four years.

Mrs. S. and I disliked each other intensely; she'd stand over me as I made a collect call home to tell my mother of my most recent infraction. These ranged from my not being in my cabin at taps, to smoking a cigarette, to kissing one of her sons or a boy who lived down the camp road.

I was really not that out of control, and later I learned that other girls had done things that were far worse. But I had become a whipping dog. In deference to her, Mrs. S. ran a good camp at which I was very happy and where I made lifelong friends. My mother saved some of my letters, and when I read them now, my devotion to that special, magical world is confirmed. But the year I was to become a counselor in training, I was not asked back; all of my friends would be at camp without me, and I was devastated.

My mother advised me to find another camp, which I did. I am now director of the camp I chose. And, yes, there is a bit of Mrs. S. in me."

—Susan Tomaselli Marcoux,
Notre Dame, 1965–68;
Bernadette, 1969–71 (director, 1998–present)

"At camp I learned that size isn't the only factor: desire and focus count for a lot." —Betty Harris Dunnam, *Kickapoo Kamp, 1952–55*

Some traditions were not to be toyed with, and so it was with color war. Each summer, for three or four days, it was as if a spell had been cast upon the entire camp. Even the youngest girls were keyed up with anticipation as we were teased with fake-outs that preceded the actual outbreak of war. Then, when the lines were finally drawn, nothing was more important than which team you were on and who was winning.

The competition was intense, with points awarded for every aspect of camp life. Bunks suddenly became sparklingly neat and clean. Not a word could be heard in what was normally a deafeningly noisy mess hall. Campers sang fight songs in perfect harmony, and the action on the fields and in the water was thrilling.

Always the finale was some wacky race in which every member of the team, without exception, had to participate. At Kear-Sarge, after three and a half days of competition and a complicated scoring system that few could comprehend, winning the Apache relay always seemed to hold the promise of overall victory. The afternoon of the last day of the contest was spent with girls skipping around the campus trying to keep potatoes on spoons, while others did twirling tricks with batons or canoe, rowboat, and swimming relays.

Oddly, despite the passion and intensity that engulfed every camper and counselor during the competition, the following summer very few of us would care about who had won. We could all recite the names of captains and co-captains going back four or five years, but who had won—and by how much—belonged only in the record books.

ARROWHEAD

KINIYA

"**My most cherished memory is being elected one of the color-war cheerleaders.** It was a shot of self-esteem that I never felt at home or at school. I was probably an average kid, maybe above average in some areas, but camp made me a confident person and gave me a special status in my own mind. I look upon those years as a great inspiration to what I have achieved in life."

—Elaine Haskell Kupsov,
Queen Lake, 1948–55

MYSTIC

PORT
Leslie Liedtke
Mary Curry
Erica Hoelscher
Lacy Martin

KEYSTONE

"**When I was fifteen, I was captain of the gold team for color war.** Every year, on the last night of the competition, we'd have a sing judged by some of the townspeople. There'd be a theme, and we'd write songs and teach them to our team. It was a very serious night, the defining moment in color war.

Teams usually won or lost the sing by a point or two, but they'd changed the scoring rules and my team lost by twenty-five points! I totally fell apart. I was humiliated and certain I'd let down my whole team. The head counselor, Bobbie, called me into her bunk, looked me in the eye, and told me how sorry she was that the new rules had caused this imbalance. Then she told me there was something she wanted to share with me that I could never tell the other captains or anyone else at camp. She told me what a wonderful job I had done and that if she'd ever had a daughter, she'd have wanted her to be me. That was enough for me; even losing color war the next day didn't matter, because my head counselor had let me know that I was special on a night so terrible I didn't know how I could go on. That's what camp did for one adolescent girl in the summer of 1963."

—Lois Weiner Prensky, *Bryn Mawr, 1957–66*

"And cheer as the winners go by . . ." —*Prayer of a Sportsman*

KAMAJI

"**My aide year I was the stern in the Tonk War Canoe,** and a day or two before the race Lynda Thompson asked me, 'Martha, have you thought about what you would do if you lost?' We Tonks were doing very well; I hadn't thought about how I would react if we lost the race. But her question gave me an opportunity to plan for it as a possibility.

Thirty minutes before the race, I gathered everyone together and threw out the possibility that we could decide then and there whether we were going to win . . . that crossing the finish line first did not necessarily make us winners. We talked about how working hard all term had been a victory in itself. Someone mentioned a line from 'Prayer of a Sportsman'—'and cheer as the winners go by' —and how we had a chance to live those lines we prayed so often. We ended our short meeting with a prayer and the desire to cross the finish line first.

We DID NOT cross the finish line first. It felt weird to me, the ultimate competitor, not to be stinging from the loss, and the crowd was perplexed at our celebratory response as we beat loudly on our canoe. But we were already winners in our hearts."

—Martha Maynard, *Mystic, 1972–80*

MYSTIC

WOHELO

Chapter 7

IT'S NOT GOOD-BYE, IT'S JUST SO LONG

I n the blink of an eye (could it have been eight weeks?) camp ended and we had to prepare ourselves for the toughest adjustment of all: reentry into the real world. Instead of rising to reveille, the jangling of an alarm clock would be our wake-up call. Instead of rushing to first-period canoeing, we'd be dragging our feet to first-period math. But the differences were greater than that. The intimacy of shared experiences and shared emotion could never be replicated in a world split between school and home. And the possibility of explaining the clash between my summer life and my rest-of-the-year life to anyone who didn't go to camp was so remote as to be bizarre.

GREYSTONE

Several years ago I drove to what was once rural New Hampshire, the site of my camp, where strip malls and Blockbusters have now sent the cows packing. The whole of my preteen and adolescent years had disappeared from the landscape, but never from my heart. I stood there and imagined us on the last night of summer, down at the waterfront, holding hands. We would stay up and cry all night long, swear allegiance for the rest of our lives, and continue crying through the next day. Camp was never supposed to end. How would I live for forty-four whole weeks until next year? No one in the outside world could understand me, or appreciate me, the way my camp friends did.

The last week, as trunks and duffel bags were delivered back to our bunks, signaling the unspeakable, the weather turned as dreary as we were. We were in the final countdown, and we all knew what that meant. We anticipated the final banquet, where each camper would be celebrated enthusiastically, but that was only a temporary distraction. We knew that by the end of the last night we would be consumed by the feeling of irreplaceable loss. After all, *this* had been the best summer ever.

At Kear-Sarge we would change into pajamas and robe, and then traipse to the waterfront with our bunk-mates, reverently singing songs heard only on that night.

ALOHA

"I sobbed at the train, and for weeks hated all my friends at home." —Harriet Simensky Friedland, *Birchwood, 1952–61*

Counselors would hand an unlit candle to each girl, and she had to choose whose flame would light hers. Then, to a background of inconsolable sobbing and sniffling, each bunk's designated girl walked to the end of the dock to launch a ship of friendship. When all eighteen or twenty little wooden boats ferrying candles were on the lake, and all 125 or so emotionally unstable girls with lit candles were huddled on the shoreline, the director would set fire to a chicken-wire outline of the year (which the arts-and-crafts counselors had constructed out of toilet-paper rolls, sanitary napkins, and newspaper). That signaled the end of the program, and now there was nothing left to do but cry and hug and cry some more. For the nine years I was at camp, I thought we were the only girls in the world who bid farewell with this never-to-be-forgotten ceremony. Needless to say, I was wrong.

"1930"

Last day of camp.

ROCKBROOK

NOKOMIS

"I need only one word to express why I so loved camp: FRIENDSHIP. Never again will I find friends like my camp friends. Even though they live all over the country, they are my best friends and the neatest part is that all of our mothers were, and are still, friends from camp. And now my daughter's best camp friend is the daughter of one of my best camp friends."

—Betsy Strum Ellis,
Appalachia, 1967, 1971–85

"We cried and cried and cried and begged the owners to hire tutors so we could stay all year long."

—Meta Cohen Lee, *Wayne, 1946–49*

REMEMBER THE TIMES YOU'VE HAD HERE

Remember the times you've
had here,
Remember the friendships true.
Remember the songs you've
sung here
And all the haunts so dear to you.
Remember the hills and wood-
lands
The lakes and skyline, too.
For you belong to (*name of camp*)
And (*name of camp*) belongs to
you.

LITTLE SHIPS OF FRIENDSHIP

When all those little ships of
friendship
Go sailing out to sea,
We know those little ships of
friendship
Are flagged with memories.
They sail and sail
Till they reach an island of
golden dreams come true.
Then all those little ships of
friendship
Come sailing back to you.

JULIETTE LOW

"My first night home I'd be miserable.
I didn't want to see my friends from home. I wanted to
be back at camp. My parents could never understand it:
'Why aren't you happy to be home with us? What about
television and air-conditioning?' I'd just mope around,
in a coma for three days, feeling so alone."

—Geri Pacht Goldenberg, *Kear-Sarge, 1960–72*

MYSTIC

"I found saying good-bye especially
difficult because I knew it would be totally different
when my campmates and I would meet in the city in the
fall. We were always strangely apart and disconnected
during those visits."

—Frances R. Connor, *Awanee, 1941–44*

"Even today, after all my years away from camp, it's easy to smile when I see or meet women who share the camp connection. It's almost a Cheshire Cat smile, a nod of the head, and then we grin. There's a special, secret bond deep down inside that is exclusive to those of us who have known the magic of sleepaway camp.

As a kid I always wished camp and school were reversed. Now, as a mom, I'm certain that children would be better off with longer summers so that camp could be extended. It's when my girls come home from camp that I can best measure how much they've grown up."

—Marla Fradin Gesner, *Louise, 1963–74*

PEANUT WEEK

The last week of camp, each girl pulls a peanut shell out of an oversize papier-mâché peanut prop. Each shell has had its nut removed and replaced with a slip of paper that has a camper's name printed on it. The girl whose name is inside the shell becomes your peanut and you are her shell. She's your secret pal, and all of Peanut Week is about doing sweet things and mischievous deeds directed at her. You might leave some candies on her cot or make her a lanyard, or you might french her bed. At the banquet, which is pretty much the last meal, each camper stands and tries to guess who her shell has been. Rarely is she right!

Then there's great hoopla, hugging, and carrying on as the shell stands up to reveal her identity.

—Joanne Newbold,
Newfound, 1964–68

ILLAHEE

GAYWOOD

"I'm eighty-two, and my dearest friend from camp lives on the next block. We continue to celebrate our birthdays together."

—Audrey Green Friedman, *Mitchell-Harlee, 1924–40*

"The whole year, no matter what went wrong at home or in school or with my friends, I knew everything would be okay when I got to camp. On every level, I was so much happier at camp; all winter I lived for it. If someone asked me, 'What are you doing this summer?' I'd look at them as though they were from Mars. 'I'm going to camp,' I'd say. 'That's where I go after school's finished. Then I come home and go to school until it's time to go back to camp.' To this day, I vacation on the lake in Maine that my camp is on. That first swim of the summer is always transporting. Camp remains alive inside of me."

—Toby Boyer Freeman, *Mataponi, 1962–72*

WYONEGONIC

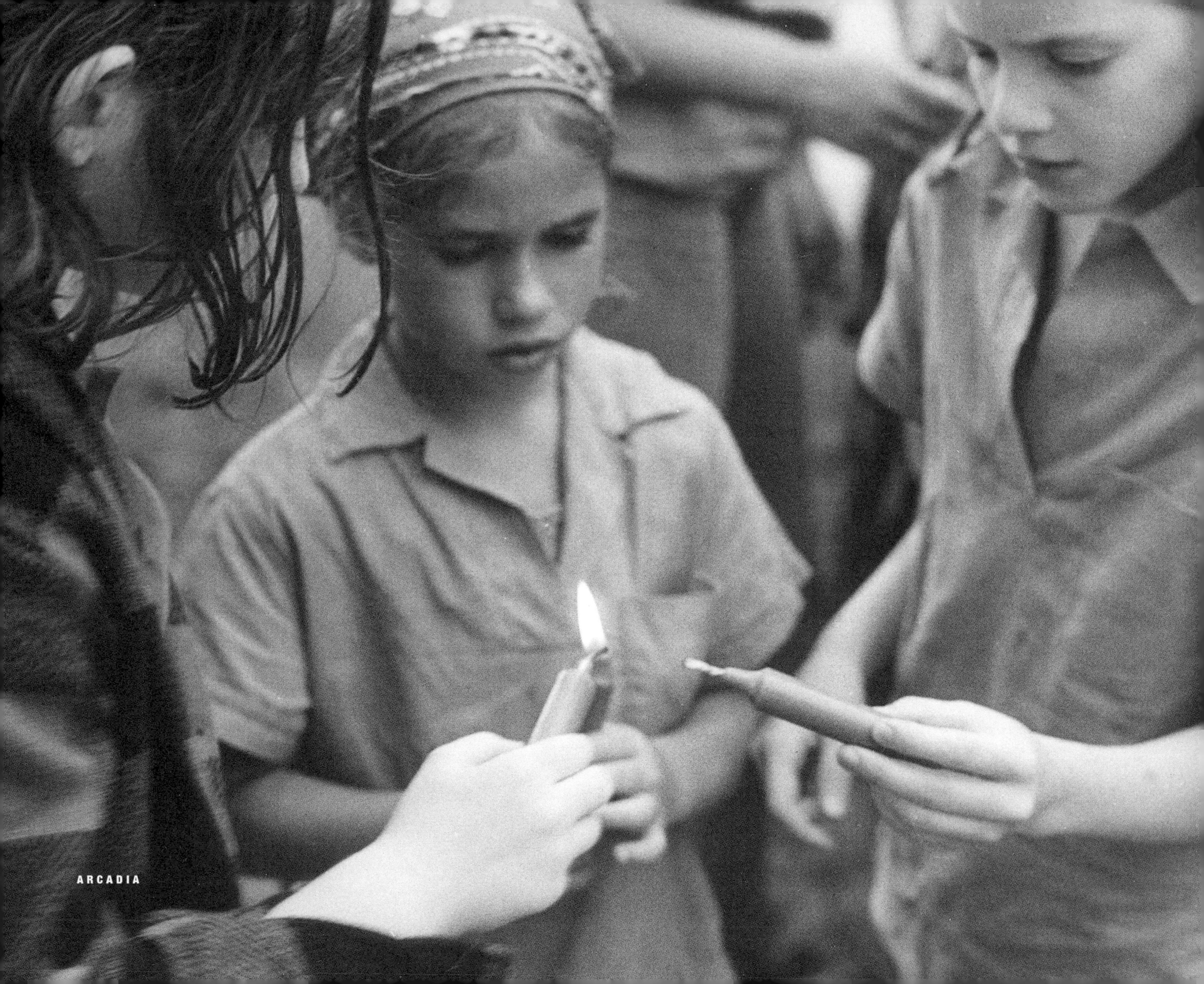
ARCADIA

"**Those days in our childhoods** were spent as they were meant to be: long days of daydreaming; sharing dreams and fears in utter sincerity; time to grow physically, mentally, and spiritually; opportunities to watch tadpoles transform themselves, stones try to turn into jelly, and dragonflies stretch their gossamer wings above velvet waters that reflected the very face of God.

Today I am, perhaps, more careful. I have learned the lessons of growing up through some pain of rejection, failure, and misplaced dreams. I have not always remembered the lessons I learned long ago on the Guadalupe River under the care and attention of those who were as needy and as unfamiliar with the world at large as I was. But these things call me. They call me back to a time when I first began to see, and they signal to me that it is time to revisit those long-ago messages and put into practice the meaning of their values. *Be ye kind to one another . . . Knock and it shall be opened unto you . . . We are molded by those that have loved us . . .*

My childhood dreams were that I would never have to leave camp. I wished for it always to be summer. Whether it was fate or the intentions of my unconscious, I made my home, ultimately, a few miles from Mystic's front door."

—Claudia Latimer Sullivan, *Mystic, 1964–79*

MICHIGAMME

CAMP FIRSTS

Wearing a uniform

Using soup cans as rollers

Feeling as though you had sisters

Meeting girls from other countries

Making decisions on your own

Using sealing wax

A kiss

A French kiss

Shaving, then walking around with bits
of Kleenex stuck to your shinbone

Cigarettes

Tampons

Beer

WHAT MATTERED

Being a returning camper

Being a second- or third- or fourth-
generation camper

Courage

Having a flashlight that worked

WHAT DIDN'T MATTER

Age (though seniors were the coolest)

Mirrors

What you wore

Grades

"I met girls who will someday be in my wedding."
—Tanishia Bailey, *Chimney Corners, 1997–01*

WALDEN

_____ MORE DAYS OF VACATION

_____ more days of vacation
Then we go to the station
Back to civilization
I (DON'T!) want to go home
I (DON'T!) want to go home
I (DON'T!) want to go home
Back to mother and father
Back to sister and brother
Back to somebody other
I (DON'T!) want to go home

WE LOVE YOU

We love you, (*name of recipient*),
   oh yes we do;
We love you, (*name of recipient*),
   and we'll be true.
When you're not near us, we're blue.
Oh, (*name of recipient*), we love you!

THE MORE WE GET TOGETHER

The more we get together, together,
   together,
The more we get together, the happier
   we are.
For your friends are my friends, and my
   friends are your friends;
The more we get together, the happier
   we are.

I'D LIKE TO LINGER

Oo . . . oo . . . oo . . . oo I'd like to
   linger
Oo . . . oo a little longer
Oo . . . oo a little longer with you.
Oo . . . oo . . . oo . . . oo it's such a
   perfect night,
Oo . . . oo it doesn't seem quite right
Oo . . . oo that this should be our last
   with you.
Oo . . . oo . . . oo . . . oo and when
   we say 'good-bye'
Oo . . . oo it's not the time to cry,
Oo . . . oo it's not good-bye,
   it's just so long.
Oo . . . oo . . . oo . . . oo and when
   September comes
Oo . . . oo we'll think of all
   the fun
Oo . . . oo of dear old (*name of camp*)
   and you.
Oo . . . oo . . . oo . . . oo.

MAKE NEW FRIENDS

(*Sing as a round.*)
Make new friends, but keep the old
One is silver and the other's gold.

ASH GROVE

Down yonder green valley where
   streamlets meander
When twilight is fading, I pensively roam.
Or at the bright noontide in solitude
   wander,
Amid the dark shades of the lonely ash
   grove.
'Tis there where the blackbird is cheerfully
   singing,
Each warbler enchants with his notes
   from a tree.
Ah, then little think I of sorrow or sadness,
The ash grove enchanting spells beauty
   for me.

KUM BA YAH

Kum ba yah, my Lord, kum ba yah,
Kum ba yah, my Lord, kum ba yah,
Kum ba yah, my Lord, kum ba yah,
Oh Lord, kum ba yah.

Someone's singing, Lord, kum ba yah,
Someone's singing, Lord, kum ba yah,
Someone's singing, Lord, kum ba yah,
Oh Lord, kum ba yah.

Other verses:
Someone's crying, Lord
Someone's praying, Lord

WYONEGONIC

"**The camp director met with all of the counselors** to select the campers who would be celebrated as 'good Indians.' There'd be a bonfire on the beach, and girls who had demonstrated leadership and friendliness were rewarded by being given Indian names. Mine was Fleeting Doe. The joy of this moment is so clear to me, it's hard to believe I'm talking about 1944."

—Lois Baum Lasky, *Lakeland, 1942–46*

ROBINDEL

ARCADIA

"**Every summer, on the last night of camp,** everyone was given a little wooden boat with a candle on it. One by one we walked to the end of the waterfront dock and had our candle lit by our counselor's candle. Then we'd set our boat afloat as we made a silent wish. Mine was the same every year: 'Please let me have breasts by next summer.'"

—Alice Jeanne Glick Meshbane, *O-Tahn-Agon, 1965–68*

Chapter 8

AND WHY WE WENT

As I drove around the country, talking to women about camp, asking them why it had meant so much to them, I heard many of the same responses: "I was a different person, a different self, at camp" . . . "I learned everything about everything at camp" . . . "At camp I was the best person I have ever been." All of this was possible because at camp everyone started off even. It didn't matter what kind of car your parents drove or what grades you earned at school or where you shopped for clothes. Our friendships were pure. And, let us not forget, girls ruled.

In this rarefied, remarkably intimate world, each of us discovered that we weren't the only one struggling with questions of identity and mixed-up feelings, that we weren't alone in going through difficulties with parents and siblings. At camp, we could explore all these things

ILLAHEE

without fear of being judged. We could also experiment with being someone other than who we were at home. It was safe.

Maybe that's why it was at camp that I learned what love is, how to be a friend, how to stand up for myself. I learned what sort of person I was—and what sort I wanted to be. I actually believe that it was at camp that I learned how to be happy. And while every summer was unique, each felt like a chapter in the same book. When I left after my last summer, it seemed as though I was ending something I had begun when I was nine.

ARCADIA

"I was afflicted with the opposite of homesickness; I had a serious case of 'camp sickness.' The day I came home, I'd make a calendar marking the days till the next summer. I spoke very little about my camp experiences, certain my friends wouldn't be able to relate, and I didn't want to give them any opportunity to criticize something I held so sacred.

Strangely enough, I don't remember what I liked best about camp. Maybe everything. It was total acceptance, an environment where I could learn, explore, and be noticed for my achievements. Home life, while not bad, wasn't particularly affirming, and as a slow developer I was ribbed a lot by the boys. I didn't fit in very well because I was more interested in sports than in boys, more interested in adventure than in makeup. I didn't get a lot of guidance at home, so I remember feeling somewhat at loose ends, whereas at camp, in a structured, achievement-oriented environment, I flourished.

I may give my camp experiences more credit than they deserve. But from my perspective, I am who I am because of having gone to camp."

—Holly Louise Carlisle,
Kineowatha, 1966, 1968–74

KEYSTONE

"**Camp provided me a stage** on which many roles could be tried and kept or discarded, as well as a haven where I was able to learn a set of core values that would follow me into adulthood. During my teen summers I learned how to experiment with my identity in the safety of an all-girls environment. One year I became a vegetarian; another year I stopped shaving my legs.

The summer I was sixteen, I learned about sex while reading *Everything You Always Wanted to Know About Sex —But Were Afraid to Ask* by flashlight under the covers, and about commitment to a goal while taking an early-morning senior lifesaving course in the freezing lake water. I learned that being there, in the woods, was more important than arriving on schedule, and that singing with female voices around a campfire is a powerful, almost magical experience. I also learned that soul mates found at camp can endure time and distance, and last a lifetime.

Try as I might, I just couldn't explain the adventure of a summer camp in the Blue Ridge Mountains to my friends back home. But not a spring goes by when I don't long to be at camp. Like Peter Pan, I never want to grow up if it means having to leave my camp experiences behind."

—Patricia "Trish" Richardson Mann,
Green Cove, 1968–74, 1976–80, 1986

"**I was the oldest of twelve children at home, always working, helping out**. But at camp, which was only one week a year, life slowed down and I got to start learning who *I* was and what *I* was interested in. I learned about nature and the serenity of the woods. I took time to hear the crickets chirp and to look into the stars and dream."

—Linda Story Mancusi, *Shawadassee, 1961–62*

MYSTIC

Sing  Along

Friends, friends, friends
We will always be.
No matter how fair or how
    stormy the weather,
(*Name of camp*) will keep us
    together.
Through all the years, filled
    with smiles and tears,
We'll stand by together, in all
    kinds of weather;
We're friends, friends, friends.

TRIPP LAKE

KEYSTONE

"**I'm a hugger and a toucher,** and I find that's not necessarily the norm. A lot of people are very protective of their space, and every once in a while it flashes through my mind: 'Oh, she must not have gone to camp.'"

—Amy Chester, *Kear-Sarge, 1959–68*

"**Camp gave me, a girl from Brooklyn,** the opportunity to learn how to ride a horse, to swim, to play tennis and volleyball, and to be selected as the all-around athlete for several years. In fact, my early start with sports resulted in my becoming a four-letter (wo)man in high school and college."

—Shelda Kahn Salvi,
Pinehurst, 1938; Towanda, 1939–40;
Wayne, 1941; Blue Ridge, 1942–47

KREADIR

MYSTIC

"**I grew up in a preppy suburb** and went to a high-pressure private school, at which I always felt awkward and stupid. I rarely played with kids besides my (somewhat annoying) siblings. I was a bit of a loner. We belonged to a club where everything was competitive.

Coming to camp was a balm for my spirit. I may have been out of step with my hometown, but I was in step with camp. I felt encouraged and comfortable and free to really explore who I was. I plumbed the depths of my own courage and will, and learned to be a friend in the truest sense. I learned that I was a better person than I believed I was."

—Christine Amiot Carter, *Green Cove, 1969–79*

THIRTEEN CRUCIAL LESSONS LEARNED AT CAMP

Having clean, dry underwear and socks is more important than clean, dry hair.

If your camera isn't loaded or charged, you have no chance of getting the shot you crave.

Hot water comes to she who showers first.

Happiness is not contingent on luxury.

It is possible that other people's parents are crazier than your own.

Giving someone a second chance is a kindness. Receiving a second chance is a gift.

Honesty is always easier than deceit.

Water does not come from a tap.

No one can be successful all the time. Sometimes, despite our best efforts, we fail.

No one knows all the answers. The fun lies in hunting for them.

Achievement is self-produced, but that doesn't always reduce the need for recognition.

Just because you "did it last year" doesn't mean you have to do it now.

Not everyone does it the way I do it.

GLEN BERNARD SLOGAN

THE BEST OF EACH FOR THE GOOD OF ALL.

TRIPP LAKE

"Our highest honor was 'Firelighter.'
It meant that you were thoughtful of others' comfort and happiness, sincere in your thought and purpose, and had the imagination to see a thing that needed to be done and the initiative to do it. I'll never forget a counselor named Helen telling me that I had missed being selected by one vote. She talked to me to encourage me to continue being an exemplary camper, and I won that award the next year. That was how I discovered goal setting, which has been a major part of my life. Later on, I made out a six-page list of goals to accomplish in my lifetime, and at sixty-one I've done just about all of them."

Betty Harris Dunnam, *Kickapoo Kamp, 1952–55*

"Camp provided the security of knowing that I could venture farther than my hometown and find new friends, new experiences and succeed. For a ten-year-old to learn that everyone was not Catholic and Southern was a really enlightening experience."

—Deborah Parker Gibbs, *Green Cove, 1968–79*

MYSTIC

GIRLS VACATION FUND CAMP

"One day in front of Bunk 1, I met Cynthia Bossowick, who became my friend for life. Each year we'd return to camp together for another round. Many years later, when I was getting divorced after twenty-nine years of marriage, Cynthia died. I had to wonder which catastrophe I took harder."

—Vicki Campbell-McNutt, *Louise, 1945–59*

"The friends I made at camp are people who have had the greatest impact on my life. I roomed with some of them at university and still stay in close touch with most of them to this day. As a matter of fact, my cabin counselor at GBC ended up being maid of honour at my wedding twelve years later."

—Mary Milne Marshall, *Glen Bernard, 1978–99*

UNIDENTIFIED

ILLAHEE

"I felt invisible at home and invisible at school.** But at camp I felt at peace with myself and with everyone else. I was encouraged and coached by vibrant women, in all shapes, sizes, and personalities, none of whom had notions about how I should act or who I should be. I can't imagine who I would be today without those many years of Girl Scout camp."

—Tara Collingwood Beuscher, *Tahigwa, Conestoga, 1974–78*

ILLAHEE

"**From the time I was twelve,** my parents came up with everything under the sun to get me not to go back to camp. But camp was my heaven and my escape, the place where I felt genuinely happy and free. I knew there would be time in my life for travel, but there'd never again be time for camp. Miserable beds, small bathrooms, and wonderful friendships: I'd never trade those summers for anything in the world."

—Susan Rifkin Karon, *Matoaka, 1969–79*

MYSTIC

HEART O' THE HILLS

13

Look into people
not just
at them

ILLAHEE

"To this day, I love waking up in a room with other women, friends, sisters, while camping or staying in a hotel together. Truly, nothing makes me happier than starting the day off with a good chat and a laugh. And I learned that at camp."

—Betsy Perry Danforth, *Kehonka, 1966–73*

"I came from an economically poor, undereducated background. But at camp, with girls from middle- and upper-income families, we were all equal. We lived together in a tent. No one knew how I lived outside of this world. I was accepted for who I was; what I had, or didn't have, didn't matter. Those friends made me feel great about myself, and without knowing it they encouraged me to reach beyond what I thought were my boundaries."

—Patricia J. Kirk Kurz, *Nomoko, 1960–65*

PINECLIFFE

TON-A-WANDAH

TAPAWINGO

"Sometimes, when I can't sleep, I mentally take a walk through camp: from bunk to bunk, to the lake and over to the boating dock. Then I try to remember as many names and faces as I can."

—Carol Oelbaum Tendler, *Nawita, 1943–49*

GIRLS VACATION FUND CAMP

"I equate camp with the freedom to just be me. There's never been another time in my life where I could be as comfortable in who I am, and let the world know about it, than those summers at camp."

—Lynn Cohodus Stahl, *Nicolet, 1953–59, 1961*

ROBINDEL

WE-HA-KEE

"The question is not do I remember, but rather how could I ever forget."

—Marnie Blayne Belkin, *Ken-Wood*, 1978–95

WALDEN

"'A' my name is Alice" A rhyming alliterative game usually played with a pinky (Spalding ball) on the bunk porch. While bouncing the ball, each player creates sentences going through the alphabet as she swings her leg over the ball at the mention of each word that begins with the letter she is up to. For example: A (*swing*) my name is Amy (*swing*) and my husband's name is Arthur (*swing*). We live in Alabama (*swing*) and we sell apples (*swing*). B (*swing*) my name is Barbara (*swing*) and my husband's name is Burt (*swing*). We live in Boston (*swing*) and we sell balloons (*swing*) . . .

big sister An older camper assigned to (or chosen by) a younger girl to provide support and advice that make camp, and growing up in general, a less daunting enterprise.

buddy A swimming companion of similar ability with whom you enter and leave the water. When the waterfront director blows her whistle and shouts "Buddies!" you quickly find your buddy and join your hands in the air.

buddy system The way in which the waterfront staff keeps track of campers in the water.

bull session A get-together where everyone shares what's on her mind. Not to be confused with a bitch session.

bunk gifts Presents brought on visiting day by a camper's parents for all her bunkmates.

bunk night An evening activity chosen by each bunk to do together as a unit. (See *bunk-o*.)

bunk-o A rainy-day activity consisting of hanging out in the bunk, reading trashy magazines, telling dirty jokes, playing games, and plucking hairs out of your legs with tweezers. Younger campers play jacks, write letters, and have storytime.

buttinksy Someone who interrupts or meddles.

canteen The place where campers shop for candy, stamps, and other necessities.

care package A present sent to camp, usually by a family member. The only kind that really matters contains contraband edibles, perhaps mailed inside a hollowed-out book.

cribs Sections of the waterfront, delineated by ability.

D-liver D-letter D-sooner D-better A message written on envelopes; perhaps an outgrowth of the belief, common at camp, that one can encourage one's teammates—in this case, the U.S. Postal Service—to ever faster speeds.

dead man's float A floating position in which the swimmer is face down on the water's surface.

deck tennis A game in which a small ring is tossed back and forth over a net, played at camp as well as on board ocean liners. Also called *tennequoits*.

dough boy Bisquick wrapped around a stick and then toasted over a campfire.

humazoo A round disk kazoo; not as loud as a traditional kazoo.

"I'll bring you an 'S'" The promise made by a person leaving camp that she will bring you a surprise upon her return.

"I've never . . ." A game in which everyone playing begins by holding up ten fingers. One girl begins by saying, "I've never blah-blahed," and whoever has done the thing that the other girl hasn't puts down a finger. You're out when you have all ten fingers down. Some girls play the reverse: put one finger down if they haven't done it, either.

J stroke An important canoe stroke in which the paddle is inserted in the water and then drawn back in the shape of the letter "J."

jelly roll The extra blanket at the foot of your bed.

Newcomb A form of volleyball in which the ball is caught and thrown rather than hit.

O.D. A counselor who patrols the area around your bunk after lights out and before counselor curfew; from *on-duty*.

progressive supper A meal in which you trek from location to location to pick up each course.

Railway Express System by which trunks and duffel bags were transported to camp—and frequently lost en route. Today UPS and Fed Ex do most of the business.

rec hall/lodge The center of camp activity.

sleepaway A special summer place where groups of girls come together to experience life in the outdoors, away from their families, while growing up in ways they never could have imagined— mentally, physically, socially, and spiritually. A special summer place that women who were girls at camp never forget, and against which they compare and measure all other experiences.

S.W.A.K. A message, signifying "Sealed With A Kiss"; usually written on the back of an envelope and often accompanied by a lipstick kiss.

swirling Putting a girl's head in the toilet and flushing.

tetherball A game in which a ball is suspended from a pole by a slender rope. A player serves by throwing the ball in one direction. The other player, standing on the other side of the pole, tries to hit the ball back in the opposite direction. They continue knocking it back and forth, each trying to keep the ball going in her direction so that the rope wraps completely around the pole.

train letters Farewell missives written on the last day of camp, meant to be read (and cried over) on the trip home.

"Truth or Dare?" A game in which the first player asks the girl whose turn it is, "Truth or Dare?" If the girl picks Truth, she has to answer any question that the first player asks. If she picks Dare, she has to do a dare. If she refuses, she's given a second choice and then a third, but there's no way out of the third and the dares usually get worse. That girl then gets to ask someone else, and the game continues until all have been asked: "Truth or Dare?"

zip line A wire or rope stretched between two points, crossed by holding on to a bar attached to a pulley.

ALOHA

ACKNOWLEDGMENTS

Even though I knew that voices other than mine would amplify my belief in the enduring influence of all-girl camps, I had no idea how many people I would need to craft this book. An endeavor like this can be successful only if passionate people are willing to share their thoughts, their histories, and their memorabilia.

For providing me with access to their archives and alumni, as well as to themselves, my boundless thanks go to: Toni Hall @ Aloha; Anne Fritts and Louise Henderson @ Arcadia; Katie Miller Warrington @ Greystone; Nicia Oakes and Sandra "Schmitty" Schmitt @ Honey Creek; Kathy and Mike Jay @ Kamaji; Tweety Eastland and Jeanne Stacy @ Mystic; Jo Stevens @ Natarswi; Pam Cobb @ Runoia; Billy and Judy Haynes @ Ton-A-Wandah; Wendy S. Cohen @ Walden; Shannon Donovan-Monti @ Chimney Corners; Sunny Moore @ Clearwater; Eva Lewandowski @ Girls Vacation Fund, Inc.; Nancy Bell @ Green Cove; Jane Ragsdale @ Heart O' The Hills; Elizabeth Tindall @ Illahee; Sue Ives and Page Ives Lemel @ Keystone; Bimmie Findlay @ Kickapoo Kamp; Marilyn Williams @ Kiniya; Roberta "Bobbie" Miller @ Louise; Mike Nathanson @ Matoaka; Ann and Nat Greenfield @ Robindel; Nancy Brenner and Leslie Levy @ Tripp Lake; Meg Clark and Miles Horton @ Waldemar; Nancy Burns @ Waukeela; Sister Arturo Cranston @ We-Ha-Kee; Louise Gulick Van Winkle @ Wohelo; Ginny Geyer, Kendall Lione Gleason, Carol Sudduth, and Steven Sudduth @ Wyonegonic. And I want to particularly recognize and thank Jane Lichtman @ Tapawingo for sharing her photo archives.

Other camp owners, camp directors, and camp mavens guided me and added to my appreciation of the sleepaway phenomenon. Many thanks to: Bernadette Dodge and her band of archivists @ Trent University; Nancy Pennell and Posie Taylor @ Aloha and Aloha Hive; Joan "Bubbles" Jost, Grace Wilson, and Dana Aumann @ Alleghany; Mackie King and Claire King @ Fernwood & Fernwood Cove; Anne Derber @ Manito-Wish YMCA; Adam Boyd @ Merri Mac; Susan Newbold Smith and Amy Sparkman @ Newfound; Dick Courtiss and Jennifer Kraft @ Vega; Toni M. Baughman @ Carysbrook; Nancy Frankel @ Farnsworth; Bob Hanson @ Farwell; Sunny Cloward and Rob Schultz @ Indian Brook; Anne Trufant @ Kahdalea; Marty Silverman @ Kippewa; Sandy Cohen and Jody Bradley-Ruby @ Marimeta; Dan Isdaner @ Mataponi; Georgianna Starz @ Nicolet; Susan Lifter @ Pinecliffe; Hoby Rosen @ Point O' Pines; Sarah Rolley and Robin Rolley Thies @ Red Pine; and Naomi Levine @ Greylock.

I was thrilled and surprised that Kear-Sarge girls, now women, still take as much pleasure as I do in remembering our summers and the inimitable Rhoda and Lee Booth. Special thanks to: Judi Kahn Zukor, Linda Levenson Geller, Nancy Cummins Silverman, Ronni

QUANSET

GLEN MOHR

Crystal Brenner, and Nancy Feingold Palmer, as well as to Maxine Lee Booth, Ruthanne Carp Schlesinger, Nancy Edman Feldman, Amy Chester, Ruth Gordon Hinerfeld, Marcelle Harrison, Judy Harmon Brezniak, Audrey Levine Lamkin, Judith Liben, Betty Liben Goldstein, Vickie Lieberman Desatnick, Jane Liberman Lundy, Bobbi Lowe, Edith Maltz Miller, Susan Moldof Rubin,

Toni Moore, Geri Pacht Goldenberg, Nancy Rosen Howren, Rena Steinberg Plost, Mary Subin Helfer, Chicky Waxler Chester, Madi Winston Greenberg, and Joan Zimmon Weinbaum. And my gratitude to Rosalie and Milton Coven, who insisted that Mara attend Kear-Sarge for many years despite her continued nonchalance.

I want to thank every woman who participated in this project for teaching me about the sleepaway dynamic. By snail mail, phone, fax, and e-mail, friends told friends, mothers told daughters (and vice versa), camp directors provided alumni addresses, and John Tanasychuk at the *Sun-Sentinel* and Vicki Miazga at the *Lakeland Times* gave me such extraordinary visibility that today there are hundreds of women whose names are not printed on the pages of this book even though they wrote or spoke eloquently of their experiences at camp.

Thanks as well to: Molly Haskell; Leigh Montville and Linda Rice at Condé Nast; Jean Baker Miller at the Stone Center, Wellesley College; Claudia

Sullivan; Virginia Messer at Eakin Press; Jocelyn Palm for helping me find John Gilchrist; Joanna Jordan and the crew at Central Talent Booking for their never-say-die spirit; Ruthellen Josselson; Marc Jacobson and Alan Mansfield at Greenberg, Traurig; Mike Avery, my computer tutor; Lily Rothman, whose contributions to this book verge on coauthorship; Brooke Bindeman Kahn; Fran Taubman; Lillian Kimbell; Pam Beall, for sharing her knowledge about song credits; Ellen Geiger and Anna at Curtis Brown for giving it the old college try; Ash DeLorenzo; Ira Chynsky; Mark Steinmetz for his eye and his patience; and Jenny Feder.

And finally, incalculable thanks to my beloved Amy Gross for overcoming her feelings about camp long enough to introduce me to Suzie Bolotin, my editor at Workman, who encouraged me to include humor and oddball whimsy in the book. The fact that the book reads as though English is my first language is a tribute to her writing and editorial skills. From our first meeting, Suzie understood my vision and managed to help me focus and refocus it so that today the book is more perfect than I ever imagined possible. Lynn Strong did a masterful job at copy editing and at making sure I wrote what I meant; the book is so much better for her involvement. Thanks also to Megan Nicolay for keeping tabs on everything.

For the two years I worked on put-

ting *Sleepaway* together, I always wondered how it would be transformed from my own obsessive project into a tapestry of voices and pictures. That's why the real hero of this whole process has to be Barbara Balch, the book's designer, who took all the pieces I'd collected, listened to all the ideas, and came back with a treasure. Working with her was confirmation of why I prefer to work as a "we" more than a "me"; it was the best. Additionally, I'm grateful to art director Paul Gamarello, whose wisdom and guidance are visible throughout the book. And no production team will ever top the concentration and tireless devotion that Doug Wolf, Barbara Peragine, and Patrick Borelli gave to this project. Their caring and imaginative collaboration allows the book to be more successful than I imagined possible.

And special recognition and appreciation for my dearest friends Joey Newbold, Michael Hampton, and Robin Dobson, who never once asked, "How much longer can this go on? Don't you have a due date?" Ultimately, of course, there'd be no book if it weren't for my parents, Jean and Howard, who made sure I could return, year after year, to my favorite place on earth. I am, and forever will be, grateful to them for that opportunity and have continued to love them very much, despite their insistence that I forsake Kear-Sarge to get a real job upon graduating from college.

Who knew there was life after camp?

CLEARWATER

GIRLS VACATION FUND CAMP

Abernathy, Elizabeth R. *Camp Greystone: The First Eighty Years.* 1999.

Allen, Hazel K. *Camps and Their Modern Administration.* New York: The Woman's Press, 1938.

Apter, Terri, and Ruthellen Josselson. *Best Friends: The Pleasures and Perils of Girls' and Women's Friendships.* New York: Three Rivers Press, 1998.

Bell, Carola. *The Fairy Four-Leaf: Outdoor Plays for Girls.* New York: Brentano's, 1923.

Carlson, Reynold E., Theodore R. Deppe, and Janet R. MacLean. *Recreation in American Life.* Belmont, CA: The Wadsworth Publishing Co., Inc., 1963.

Coale, Anna Worthington. *Summer in the Girls' Camp.* New York: The Century Co., 1919.

Conford, Ellen. *Hail, Hail Camp Timberwood.* Boston: Little, Brown and Co., 1978.

Davis, Anne Pence. *Mimi at Camp: The Adventures of a Tomboy.* Chicago: The Goldsmith Publishing Company, 1935.

Dimock, Hedley S., and Charles E. Hendry. *Camping and Character.* New York: Association Press, 1939.

Doty, Richard. *The Character Dimension of Camping.* New York: Association Press, 1960.

Edgar, Mary S. *Under Open Skies.* Toronto: Clarke, Irwin & Company Limited, 1962.

———. *Wood-Fire and Candle-Light.* Toronto: The Macmillan Company of Canada Limited, 1945.

Eells, Eleanor Eleanor. *Eells' History of Organized Camping: The First 100 Years.* Martinsville, IN: American Camping Association, 1986.

Gibson, H. W. "The History of Organized Camping." *The Camping Magazine,* vol. VIII, Nos. 1–9 (1936).

Graham, Abbie. *The Girls' Camp: Program Making for Summer Leisure.* New York: The Woman's Press, 1933.

Graham, Abbie. *Working at Play in Summer Camps.* New York: The Woman's Press, 1941.

Gutman, Richard J. S., and Kellie O. Gutman. *The Summer Camp Memory Book.* New York: Crown Publishers, Inc., 1983.

Hamilton, Mary G. *The Call of Algonquin: A Biography of a Summer Camp.* Toronto: The Ryerson Press, 1958.

Hill, Thomas, and Steve Slavkin. *Salute Your Shorts: Life at Summer Camp.* New York: Workman Publishing, 1986.

Lehman, Eugene H., et al. *Camps and Camping.* New York: American Sports Publishing Co., 1922, 1926, 1929.

Mason, Bernard S. *Camping and Education: Camp Problems from the Campers' Viewpoint.* New York: The McCall Company, 1930.

Mitchell, A. Viola, Ida B. Crawford, and Julia D. Robberson. *Camp Counseling.* Philadelphia: W. B. Saunders Company, 1970.

Palm, Jocelyn. *Legacy to a Camper.* Toronto: The Canadian Camping Association, 1982.

Rubin, Susan Goldman. *Emily Good as Gold.* San Diego: Browndeer Press, 1993.

Sargent, Porter. *Summer Camps: An Annual Survey.* Boston: Porter Sargent, 1932.

Sebra, Diane. *Hot Showers and Other Girls' Camp Myths.* Orem, UT: Grandin Book Company, 1995.

Soifer, Margaret K. *Firelight Entertainments: A Handbook of Campfire Programs.* New York: Association Press, 1944.

Sullivan, Claudia. *Heartfelt: A Memoir of Camp Mystic Inspirations.* Austin: Eakin Press, 2001.

———, ed. *Summer Come, Summer Go: A Collection of Memories.* Austin: Nortex Press, 1991.

Van Krevelen, Alice. *Summer Camp: A Guidebook for Parents.* Chicago: Nelson-Hall, 1981.

Wack, Henry Wellington. *The Camping Ideal: A New Human Race.* New York: The Red Book Magazine, 1925.

———. *More About Summer Camps: Training for Leisure.* New York: The Red Book Magazine, 1926.

Webb, Kenneth B. and Susan H. *Summer Magic: What Children Gain from Camp.* New York: Association Press, 1953.

Willett, Sue Van Noy, and Carolyn Carmichael Wheat. *The Waldemar Story: Camping in the Texas Hill Country.* Austin: Eakin Press, 1998.

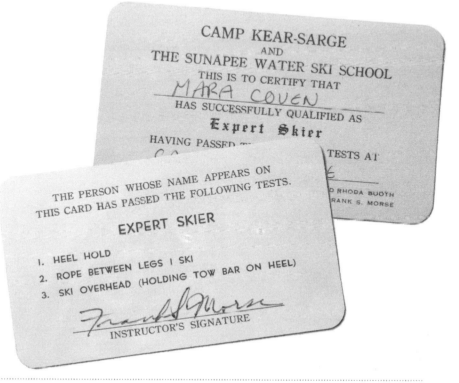

CAMP LISTING

The following list represents those camps from which I interviewed alumnae or received photographs or memorabilia.

Abena, Belgrade Lakes, Maine

Abnaki Girl Scout Camp, North Hero, Vermont

Akiba, Bartonsville, Pennsylvania

Ak-O-Mak, Ahmic Harbour, Ontario, Canada

Alford Lake, Hope, Maine

Alice Merritt, East Hartford, Connecticut

Alleghany, Lewisburg, West Virginia

Allegro, North Conway, New Hampshire

Allegro, Pittsfield, Massachusetts

Aloha, Fairlee, Vermont

Aloha Hive, Ely, Vermont

Alpine, Parksville, New York

Anawan, Meredith, New Hampshire

Anchorage, Central Valley, New York

Appalachia, Covington, Virginia

Arcadia, Casco, Maine

Arrowhead, Hunt, Texas

Awanee, Brandon, Vermont

Belvoir Terrace, Lenox, Massachusetts

Berkshire Hills, New Canaan, Connecticut

Bernadette, Wolfeboro, New Hampshire

Betsy Cox, Pittsford, Massachusetts

Beverly, Beverly, Massachusetts

Big Tree, Guerneville, California

Birch Hill, New Durham, New Hampshire

Birch Knoll, Phelps, Wisconsin

Birchmere, Antrim, New Hampshire

Birch Trail, Minong, Wisconsin

Birchwood, Brandon, Vermont

Black Hawk, Antigo, Wisconsin

Blue Ridge, Equinunk, Pennsylvania

Bonnie Brae, East Otis, Massachusetts

Broadlea, Goshen, New York

Brookwood, Glen Spey, New York

Brown Ledge, Colchester, Vermont

Bryn Mawr, Honesdale, Pennsylvania

Burnham-by-the-Sea, Newport, Rhode Island

Burr Oaks, Mukwonago, Wisconsin

Carondowanna, Beaver, Pennsylvania

Carysbrook, Riner, Virginia

Catherine Capers, Wells, Vermont

Catoctin, Lovettsville, Virginia

Chattooga, Tallulah Falls, Georgia

Che-Na-Wah, Minerva, New York

Cherokee, Saranac Inn, New York; Beach Lake, Pennsylvania

Chimney Corners, Becket, Massachusetts

Chunn's Cove, Chunn's Cove, North Carolina

Clear Lake, Chelsea, Michigan

Clearwater, Minocqua, Wisconsin

Conestoga, Davenport, Iowa

Couchiching, Longford Mills, Ontario, Canada

Cowasset, North Falmouth, Massachusetts

Crestridge, Ridgecrest, North Carolina

Crystal Lake, Eton Center, New Hampshire

Crystal Lake, Roscoe, New York

Danbee, Peru, Massachusetts

Davern, Maberly, Ontario, Canada

Delanore, Lackawaxen, Pennsylvania

Diana, Glen Spey, New York

Douglas, Pebble Beach, California

Echo, Racquette Lake, New York

Echo, Burlingham, New York

Echo Hill, Stanton Station, New Jersey

Ecole Champlain, Ferrisburg, Vermont

Edalia, Haverstraw, New York

Elliot Barker, Angel Fire, New Mexico

Evergreen, Potter Place, New Hampshire

Fair Haven, Brooks, Maine

Farnsworth, Thetford, Vermont

Farwell, Newbury, Vermont

Fern, Marshall, Texas

Fernwood, Poland, Maine

Fernwood Cove, Harrison, Maine

Fleur-De-Lis, Fitzwilliam, New Hampshire

Forest and Indian Acres Camps, Freyburg, Maine

Four Winds Girl Scout Camp, Bournedale, Massachusetts

Gaywood, Clear Lake, Iowa

Ge-Wa-Nah, White Lake, New York

Geneva, Lake Como, Pennsylvania

Girls Vacation Fund Inc., East Windham, New York

Glen Bernard, Sundridge, Ontario, Canada

Glenmere, Montery, Massachusetts

Glen Mohr Presbyterian Camp, Brechin, Ontario, Canada

Green Cove, Tuxedo, North Carolina

Greylock, Raquette Lake, New York

Greystone, Tuxedo, North Carolina

Hanoum, Thetford, Vermont

Heart O' The Hills, Hunt, Texas

Hiawatha, Kezar Falls, Maine

Hickory Hill, Edgerton, Wisconsin

Hill Manor, Kelsey, New York

Hilltop, Hancock, New York

Hitaga, Walker, Iowa

Hollywood Land, Hollywood, California

Honey Creek, Hunt, Texas

Huckins, Freedom, New Hampshire

Huntington Lake, Huntington Lake, California

Illahee, Brevard, North Carolina

Indian Brook, Plymouth, Vermont

Jeanne d'Arc, Merrill, New York

Juliette Low, Cloudland, Georgia

Junaluska, Lake Junaluska, North Carolina

Kahdalea, Brevard, North Carolina

Kamaji (formerly Kawajian), Cass Lake, Minnesota

Kear-Sarge, Elkins, New Hampshire

Kee-Wah-Ke, Wingdale, New York

Keewano, Hesperia, Michigan

Kehonka, Wolfeboro, New Hampshire

Ken-Wood, Kent, Connecticut

Keystone, Brevard, North Carolina

Kickapoo Kamp, Kerriville, Texas

Kineowatha, Wilton, Maine

Kiniya, Colchester, Vermont

Kinni Kinnic, Poultney, Vermont

Kippewa, Monmouth, Maine

Kuwiyan, Meredith, New Hampshire

Lake Hubert, Lake Hubert,
Minnesota

Lake Lure, Lake Lure, North Carolina

Lakeland, Angola, New York

Lakeside Pines, Pottersville, New York

Lake Windermere Ranch-Camp,
Invermere, British Columbia, Canada

Land O' Peaks Ranch, Estes Park,
Colorado

Laughing Loon, Little Ossipee Lake,
Maine

Laughing Water, Tuxedo, New York

Laurel, Blairstown, New Jersey

Lenore, Hinsdale, Massachusetts

Little Notch, Fort Ann, New York

Little Wohelo, South Casco, Maine

Lochearn, Post Mills, Vermont

Lokanda, Glen Spey, New York

Longacres, East Aurora, New York

Louise, Cascade, Maryland

Manito-Wish YMCA, Boulder Junction,
Wisconsin

Manitou, Central Valley, New York

Marimeta, Eagle River, Wisconsin

Mary Munger, Trussville, Alabama

Mataponi, Naples, Maine

Matoaka, Smithfield, Maine

Mawavi, Prince William Forest, Virginia

May Flather, Mt. Solon, Virginia

Merrie Woode, Sapphire, North Carolina

Merri Mac, Black Mountain,
North Carolina

Mi-A-Kon-Da, Dunchurch, Ontario,
Canada

Michigamme, Michigamme, Michigan

Mikan, Arden, New York

Milo Light Camps, Colchester,
Connecticut

Minne Wonka Lodge, Three Lakes,
Wisconsin

Mishannock, Kingston, Massachusetts

Mishnoah, Holland, Massachusetts

Mitchell, Tyler Hill, Pennsylvania

Mont Shenandoah, Millboro Springs,
Virginia

Mudjekeewis, Center Lovell, Maine

Mystic, Hunt, Texas

Nah-Jee-Wah, Milford, Pennsylvania

Nakanawa, Mayland, Tennessee

Natarswi, Millinocket, Maine

Navarac, Saranac Lake, New York

Nawita, Paradox Lake, New York

Netimus, Milford, Pennsylvania

Newaka, Ward, Colorado

Newfound, Harrison, Maine

Nicolet, Eagle River, Wisconsin

Nokomis, Mahopac, New York

Nokomis, Mercer, Wisconsin

Nomoko, Freehold, New Jersey

Northern Hills, Eagle River, Wisconsin

Northway (formerly Northway Lodge),
Algonquin Park, Ontario, Canada

Notre Dame, Munsonville, New
Hampshire

Noya River, San Jose, California

Nyoda, Oak Ridge, New Jersey

Oconto, Tichborne, Ontario, Canada

Onaway, Bridgewater, New Hampshire

Oneka, Tafton, Pennsylvania

Orinsekwa, East Berne, New York

Osoha, Boulder Junction, Wisconsin

O-Tahn-Agon, Three Lakes, Wisconsin

Owaissa, Monterey, Massachusetts

Owaissa, Pocono Pines, Pennsylvania

Pembroke, Pembroke, Massachusetts

Pesquasawasis, Poland, Maine

Pinecliffe, Harrison, Maine

Pine Hill, Center Barnstead,
New Hampshire

Point O' Pines, Brant Lake, New York

Pondicherry Kennebec Girl Scout Camp,
Bridgton, Maine

Quanset Sailing Camps, South Orleans,
Massachusetts

Queen Lake, Athol, Massachusetts

Quinibeck (Jr. & Sr.), Ely, Vermont

Raleigh, Livingston Manor, New York

Rappatak, Fryeburg, Maine

Raquette Lake, Raquette Lake, New
York

Red Pine, Minocqua, Wisconsin

Red Wing, Renfrew, Pennsylvania

Red Wing, Schroon Lake, New York

Reeta, Zieglersville, Pennsylvania

Rhoda, West Copake, New York

Robindel, Center Harbor, New
Hampshire

Rockbrook, Brevard, North Carolina

Rocky Mountain Ranch of the
Keewaydin Camps, Holland Lake
and Helmville, Montana

Romaca, Hinsdale, Massachusetts

Rondack, Pottersville, New
York

Runoia, Belgrade Lakes,
Maine

Seafarer, Arapahoe, North
Carolina

Sea Gull, Charlevoix,
Michigan

Severance, Severance, New York

Shawadassee, Lawton, Michigan

Sherwood, Pontiac, Michigan

Skyland, Clyde, North Carolina

Somerset, Oakland, Maine

Songadeewin Wigwam of the Keewaydin
Camps, Barton, Vermont

St. Vincent De Paul, Butler, New Jersey

Summit Lake, Hendersonville, North
Carolina

Sunningdale, Sebago Lake, Maine

Swatonah, Damascus, Pennsylvania

Tabor, Lake Como, Pennsylvania

Tahigwa, Dorchester, Iowa

Tanamakoon, Algonquin Park,
Huntsville, Ontario, Canada

Tapawingo, Sweden, Maine

Teela-Wooket, Roxbury, Vermont

Tegawitha, Tobyhanna, Pennsylvania

Timberline, Jewett, New York

Ton-A-Wandah, Hendersonville,
North Carolina

Tonawandah, New London,
New Hampshire

Towanda, Honesdale, Pennsylvania

Trail's End, Lexington, Kentucky

Trebor, Fryeburg, Maine

Tripp Lake, Poland, Maine

Truda, Oxford, Maine

Tu-End-O-Wee, St. Charles, Illinois

Turkey Creek Girl Scout Camp, Pratt, Kansas

Vega, Kents Hill, Maine

Wabasso, Bradford, New Hampshire

Wabanaki (Jr. & Sr.), Hillside, Maine

Wahconah, Pittsfield, Massachusetts

Wakohah, Roscoe, New York

Waldemar, Hunt, Texas

Walden, Denmark, Maine

Wapanacki, Hardwick, Vermont

Wapomeo, Algonquin Park, Huntsville, Ontario, Canada

Waukeela, Eaton Center, New Hampshire

Wawenock, Raymond, Maine

Wayne, Preston Park, Pennsylvania

Waziyatah, Waterford, Maine

We-Ha-Kee, Winter, Wisconsin

Whippoorwill, Keeseville, New York

Wicosuta, Bristol, New Hampshire

Wind-in-the-Pines, Plymouth, Massachusetts

Winnisquam, Milton, Vermont

Winona, Eagle River, Wisconsin

Winona, Lake Como, Pennsylvania

Wishe, Middletown, New York

Wohelo, South Casco, Maine

Woodlands, Bridgton, Maine

Woodmere, Paradox, New York

Wyoda, Ely, Vermont

Wyonegonic, Denmark, Maine

Yalani, Green Valley Lake, California

YMCA Camp Nokomis, Laconia, New Hampshire

Born in New York City, Laurie Susan Kahn moved to Roslyn, Long Island, as a young girl. The rest of her childhood can be measured in summers spent at Camp Kear-Sarge in Elkins, New Hampshire. Eventually, Laurie attended the University of Wisconsin. But it was not until 1987, when she was named Executive Vice President, Director of Radio and Television Production, at Young & Rubicam in New York, that she overcame her disappointment at never having been color war captain. Only then did she stop having name tapes sewn into her clothing. Laurie now bunks in Noyac, New York. If you have a camp story you'd like to share with her, please e-mail it to laurie@sleepaway.net.

Laurie Kahn
Camp Kear-Sarge